The Idyll of the White Lotus
and
The Story of Sensa

The Idyll of the White Lotus

and

The Story of Sensa

By
Mabel Collins

With a commentary on *The Idyll* by
Tallapragada Subba Rao

evertype
2022

Published by Evertype, 19A Corso Street, Dundee, DD2 1DR, Scotland. www.evertype.com.

First published in book form by John W. Lovell Co., New York 1890.

A catalogue record for this book is available from the British Library.

ISBN-10 1-78201-180-3
ISBN-13 978-1-78201-180-4

Typeset in Caslon & Caslon Openface by Michael Everson.

Design and cover design: Michael Everson. "White Lotus" © Kampwit, www.dreamstime.com/kampwit_info.

TO

THE TRUE AUTHOR,

THE INSPIRER OF THIS WORK,

IT IS DEDICATED.

Preface

The ensuing pages contain a story which has been told in all ages and among every people. It is the tragedy of the Soul. Attracted by Desire, the ruling element in the lower nature of Man. it stoops to sin; brought to itself by suffering, it turns for help to the redeeming Spirit within; and in the final sacrifice achieves its apotheosis and sheds a blessing on mankind.

Prologue

Behold I stood alone, one among many, an isolated individual in the midst of a united crowd. And I was alone, because, among all the men my brethren who knew, I alone was the man who both knew and taught. I taught the believers at the gate, and was driven to do this by the power that dwelleth in the sanctuary. I had no escape, for in that deep darkness of the most sacred shrine, I beheld the light of the inner life, and was driven to reveal it, and by it was I upheld and made strong. For indeed, although I died, it took ten priests of the temple to accomplish my death, and even then they but ignorantly thought themselves powerful.

Table of Contents

The Idyll of the White Lotus

Book I

Chapter I

Ere my beard had become a soft down upon my chin I entered the gates of the temple to begin my novitiate in the order of the priesthood.

My parents were shepherds outside the city. I had never but once entered within the city walls until the day my mother took me to the gate of the temple. It as a feast day in the city, and my mother, a frugal and industrious woman thus fulfilled two purposes by her journey. She took me to my destination, and then she departed to enjoy a brief holiday amid the sights and scenes of the city.

I was enthralled by the crowds and noises of the streets. I think my nature was always one that strove to yield itself to the great whole of which it was such a small part—and by yielding itself, to draw back into it the sustenance of life.

But out of the bustling throng we soon turned. We entered upon a broad, green plain upon the further side of which ran our sacred, beloved river. How plainly I behold that scene still! On the banks of the water I saw the sculptured roofs and glittering ornaments of the temple and its surrounding buildings shining in the clear morning air. I had no fear, for I had no definite expectations. But I wondered much whether life within those gates was as beautiful a thing as it seemed to me it must be.

At the gate stood a black-robed novice speaking to a woman from the city, who carried flasks of water which she urgently prayed one of the priests to bless. She would then have for sale a precious burden—a thing paid dearly for by the superstitious populace.

I peeped through the gate as we stood waiting for our turn of speech, and beheld a sight that struck me with awe. That awe lasted a long time, even when I had entered into almost hourly familiarity with the figure which so impressed me.

It was one of the white-robed priests, pacing slowly down the broad avenue towards the gate. I had never seen one of those white-robed priests before, save on the single occasion when I had before visited the city. I then had seen several upon the sacred boat in the midst of a river procession.

But now this figure was near me, approaching me—I held my breath.

The air was indeed very still, but those stately white garments looked, as the priest moved beneath the shadow of the avenue, as if no earthly breeze could stir them. His step had the same equable character. He moved, but it seemed scarcely as though he walked in the fashion that other and impetuous mortals walk. His eyes were bent on the ground, so that I could not see them; and, indeed, I dreaded the raising of those drooping lids. His complexion was fair, and his hair of a dull gold colour. His beard was long and full, but it had the same strangely immovable, almost carven look, to my fancy. I could not imagine it blown aside. It seemed as though cut in gold, and made firm for eternity. The whole man impressed me thus—as a being altogether removed from the ordinary life of man.

The novice looked around, his notice attracted probably by my intense gaze, for no sound reached my ears from the priest's footfall. "Ah!" he said, "here is the holy priest Agmahd, I will ask him."

Closing the gate behind him, he drew back, and we saw him speak to the priest, who bowed his head slightly. The man returned, and taking the water flasks from the woman carried them to the priest, who laid his hand for a second upon them.

She took them again with profuse thanks, and then we were asked our business.

I was soon left alone with the black-robed novice. I was not sorry though considerably awed. I had never cared much for my old task of tending my father's sheep, and of course I was already filled with the idea that I was about to become something different from the common herd of men. This idea will carry poor human nature through severer trials even than that of leaving one's home forever and entering finally upon a new and untried course of life.

The gate swung to behind me, and the black-robed man locked it with a great key that hung to his waist. But the action gave me no sense of imprisonment—only a consciousness of seclusion and separateness. Who could associate imprisonment with a scene such as that which lay before me?

The temple doors were facing the gate, at the other end of a broad and beautiful avenue. It was not a natural avenue formed by trees planted in the ground, and luxuriating in a growth of their own choosing. It was formed by great tubs of stone, in which were planted shrubs of enormous size, but evidently trimmed and guided most carefully into the strange shapes they formed. Between each shrub was a square block of stone, upon which was a carven figure. Those figures nearest the gate I saw to be sphinxes and great animals with human heads but afterwards I did not dare raise my eyes to gaze curiously upon them; for I saw again approaching us, in the course of his regular walk to and fro, the golden-bearded priest Agmahd.

Walking on by the side of my guide, I kept my eyes upon the ground. When he paused I paused, and found that my eyes fell upon the hem of the priest's white robe. That hem was delicately embroidered with golden characters: it was enough to absorb my attention and fill me with wonder for a while.

"A new novice?" I heard a very quiet and sweet voice say. "Well, take him into the school; he is but a youth yet. Look up, boy; do not fear."

I looked up, thus encouraged, and encountered the gaze of the priest. His eyes, I saw, even then in my embarrassment, were of changing colour—blue and gray. But, soft-hued though they were, they did not give me the encouragement which I had heard in his voice. They were calm indeed: full of knowledge: but they made me tremble.

He dismissed us with a movement of his hand, and pursued his even walk down the grand avenue; while I, more disposed to tremble than I had been before, followed silently my silent guide. We entered the great central doorway of the temple, the sides of which were formed of immense blocks of uncut stone. I suppose a fit of something like fear must have come upon me, after the inquisition of the holy priest's eyes; for I regarded these blocks of stone with a vague sense of terror.

Within I saw that from the central doorway, a passage proceeded in a long direct line with the avenue through the building. But that was not our way. We turned aside and entered upon a network of smaller corridors, and passed through some small bare rooms upon our way.

We entered at last a large and beautiful room. I say beautiful, though it was entirely bare and unfurnished, save for a table at one corner. But its proportions were so grand, and its structure so elegant, that even my eye, unaccustomed to discern architectural beauties, was strangely impressed, with a sense of satisfaction.

At the table in the corner sat two other youths, copying or drawing, I could not quite see what. At all events I saw they were very busy, and I wondered that they scarcely raised their heads to observe our entrance. But, advancing, I perceived that behind one of the great stone projections of the wall, there sat an aged white-robed priest, looking at a book which lay upon his knee.

He did not notice us until my guide stood deferentially bowing right in front of him.

"A new pupil?" he said, and looked keenly at me out of his dim, bleared-looking eyes. "What can he do?"

"Not much I fancy," said my guide, speaking of me in an easy tone of contempt. "He has been but a shepherd lad."

"A shepherd lad," echoed the old priest; "he will be no use here, then. He had best work in the garden. Have you ever learned to draw or copy writing?" he asked, turning upon me.

I had been taught these things as far as might be, but such accomplishments were rare, except in the priestly schools and among the small cultivated classes outside the priesthood.

The old priest looked at my hands, and turned back to his book.

"He must learn some time," he said; "but I am too full of work now to teach him. I want more to help me in my work; but with these sacred writings that have to be closed now, I cannot stay to instruct the ignorant. Take him to the garden for a while at least, and I will see about him by-and-by."

My guide turned away and walked out of the room. With a last look around, at its beautiful appearance, I followed him.

I followed him down a long, long passage, which was cool and refreshing in its darkness. At the end was a gate instead of a door, and here my guide rang a loud bell.

We waited in silence after the bell had rung. No one came, and presently my guide rang the bell again. But I was in no hurry. With my face pressed against the bars of the gate, I looked forth into a world so logical, that I thought to myself, "It will be no ill to me if the blear-eyed priest does not want to take me from the garden yet a while!"

It had been a dusty hot walk from our home to the city, and there the paved streets had seemed to my country-bred feet infinitely wearisome. Within the gates of the temple I had as yet only passed down the grand avenue, where everything filled me so deeply, with awe, that I scarce dared look upon it. But here was a world of delicate and refreshing glory. Never had I seen a garden like this. There was greenness, deep greenness; there was a sound of water, the murmuring of gentle water under control, ready to do service for man and refresh in the midst of the burning heat which called the magnificence of colour and grand development of form into the garden.

A third time the bell rang—and then I saw, coming from among the great green leaves, a black-robed figure. How strangely out of place did the black dress look here! and I thought with consternation that I should also be clothed in those garments before long, and should wander among the voluptuous beauties of this magical place like a strayed creature from a sphere of darkness.

The figure approached, brushing, with its coarse . . ., like the delicate foliage. I gazed with a sudden awakening of interest upon the face of the man who drew near, and into whose charge I supposed I was to be committed. And well I might; for it was a face to awake interest in any human breast.

Chapter II

"What is it?" asked the man querulously, as he looked at us through the gate. "I sent fruit and to spare into the kitchen this morning. And I can give you no more flowers to-day; all I have to pluck will be wanted for the procession to-morrow."

"I am not wanting your fruit or your flowers," said my guide, who seemed fond of adopting a lofty tone. "I have brought you a new pupil, that's all."

He unlocked the gate, motioned me to pass through, and shutting it behind me, walked away down the long corridor (which now, looking back from the garden seemed so dark) without another word.

"A new pupil for me! And what am I to teach you, child of the country?" I gazed upon the strange man in silence. How could I tell what he was to teach me?

"Is it the mysteries of the growth of the plants you are to learn?—or the mysteries of the growth of sin and deceit? Nay, child, look not so upon me, but ponder my words and you will by-and-by understand them. Now, come with me, and fear not."

He took my hand and led me under the tall-leaved plants towards the sound of water. How exquisite it seemed to my ears, that soft, bright, musical rhythm!

"Here is the home of our Lady the Lotus," said the man. "Sit down here and look upon her beauty while I work; for I have much to do that you cannot help me in."

Nothing loth, indeed, was I to sink upon the green grass and only look—look in amazement—in wonder—in awe!

That water—that delicate-voiced water—lived only to feed the queen of flowers. I said to myself, thou art indeed the Queen of all flowers imaginable.

THE WHITE LOTUS.

And as I gazed dreamingly in my youthful enthusiasm upon this white bloom which seemed to me, with its soft, gold-dusted heart, the very emblem of pure, romantic love—as I gazed the flower seemed to change in shape—to expand—to rise towards me. And lo, drinking at the stream of sweet sounding water, stooping to take its refreshing drops upon her lips, I beheld a woman of fair skin with hair like the dust of gold. Amazed, I looked and strove to move towards her, but ere I could make any effort my whole consciousness left me, and, I suppose, I must have swooned away. For, indeed, the next that I can recall I lay upon the grass, with the sense of cool water upon my face, and opening my eyes, I beheld the black-robed, strange faced gardener leaning over me.

"Was the heat too much for thee?" he asked, his brow knit in perplexity. "Thou lookest a strong lad to faint for the heat, and that, moreover, in a cool place like this."

"Where is she?" was my only reply, as I attempted to rise upon my elbow and look towards the lily bed.

"What!" cried the man his whole countenance changing, and assuming a look of sweetness that I should never have supposed could appear upon a face so naturally unbeautiful. "Hast thou seen her? But no—I am hasty in supposing it. What have you seen boy?—do not hesitate to tell me."

The gentleness of his expression helped my scattered and startled senses to collect themselves. I told him what I had seen and, as I spoke, I looked towards the lily bed, hoping, indeed, that the fair woman might again stoop to slake her thirst at the streamlet.

The manner of my strange teacher gradually changed as I spoke to him. When I ceased describing the beautiful woman with the enthusiasm of a boy who has never seen any but his own dusky-skinned race, he fell upon his knees beside me.

"Thou hast seen her!" he said in a voice of deep excitement. "All hail! for thou art destined to be a teacher among us—a help to the people—thou art a seer!"

Bewildered by his words, I only looked upon him in silence. After a moment I grew terrified, for I began to think he must be mad. I looked around, wondering whether I could return to the temple and escape from him. But even as I debated within myself whether to venture upon this, he rose and turned upon me with the singular sweet smile, which appeared to cover and hide the ugliness of his strongly marked features.

"Come with me," he said; and I rose and followed him. We passed through the garden which was so full of attractions for my wandering eyes that I loitered on my path behind him. Ah, such sweet flowers; such rich purples and deep-hearted crimson. Difficult I found it not to pause and inhale the sweetness of each fair-faced blossom, though still they seemed to me, in my so recent adoration of its beauty, to but reflect the supreme exquisiteness of the white lotus flower.

We went towards a gate in the temple: a different one from that by which I had entered the garden. As we approached it, there issued forth two priests clad in the same white linen robes as I had seen worn by the golden-bearded priest Agmahd. These men were dark; and though they moved with a similar stateliness and equilibrium, as though indeed, they were the most firmly rooted growth of the earth, yet to my eyes they lacked a something which the priest Agmahd possessed—a certain perfection of calm and assuredness. They were younger than he, I soon saw; perhaps therein lay the difference. My dark-visaged teacher drew them aside, leaving me to stand in the pleasant shadow of the deep-arched doorway. He spoke to them excitedly, though evidently with reverence; while they, listening with quick interest, glanced ever and anon towards me.

Presently they came to me, and the black-robed man turned and moved over the grass, as though returning on the way we had come together. The white-clad priests, advancing under the doorway, spoke together in low whispers. When they reached me they motioned me to follow them, and I did so: passing through cool, high-roofed corridors and gazing idly, as was always a foolish habit of mine, upon everything I passed; while they, still whispering together as they preceded me, would now and then cast looks upon me, the meaning of which I could not understand.

Presently they turned out of the corridors, and entered into a large room similar to the one I had already seen where the old priest was instructing his copyists. This was divided by an embroidered curtain which fell in majestic folds from the lofty roof to the ground. I always loved beautiful things, and I noticed how, as it touched the ground, it stood firm with the stiffness of the rich gold work upon it.

One of the priests advanced, and drawing back one side of the curtain a little, I heard him say—

"My lord, may I enter?"

And now I began to tremble a little again. They had not looked unkindly upon me, yet how could I tell what ordeal awaited me? I looked in fear upon the beautiful curtain and wondered, in some natural fear, who sat behind it.

I had not overlong in which to tremble and be afraid of I knew not what. Before long the priest who had entered returned, and accompanying him I saw was the golden-bearded priest Agmahd.

He did not speak to me, but said to the others—

"Wait thou here with him, while I go to my brother Kamen Baka."

And saying this, he left us alone again in the great stone room.

My fears returned trebly upon me. Had but the stately priest given me a glance which held kindness in it, I had not so yielded to them, but now I was again plunged in vague terrors of what next should come upon me; and I was weakened also by the swoon which had but so recently prostrated me. Trembling, I sank upon a stone bench, which ran around the wall; while the two dark-haired priests talked together.

I think the suspense would soon hove brought another lapse into unconsciousness upon me, but suddenly I was again awakened to the doubts and possibilities of my position by the entrance of Agmahd, accompanied by another priest of most noble appearance. He was fair-skinned and fair-haired, though not so fair in either as Agmahd; he shared with him the stately immobility of appearance which made Agmahd an object of the deepest awe to me; and in his dark eyes there was a benevolence which I had not yet seen in any of the priests' countenances. I felt less fearful as I looked upon him.

"This is he," said Agmahd, in his musically cold voice.

Why, I wondered, was I thus spoken of? I was but a new novice, and had already been handed over to my teacher.

"Brethren" cried Kamen Baka, "is it not best that he should be clothed in the white garment of the seer? Take him to the baths; let him bathe and be anointed. Then will I and Agmahd my brother put upon him the white robe. We will then leave him to repose, while we report to the company of the high priests. Bring him back here when he has bathed."

The two younger priests led me from the room. I began to see that they belonged to an inferior order in the priesthood, and, looking on them now, I saw that their white robes had not the beautiful golden embroidery upon them, but were marked with black lines and stitchings around the edges.

How delicious, after all my weariness, was the scented bath which they led me to! It soothed and eased my very spirit. When I left it I was rubbed with a soft and sweet oil, and then they wrapped me in a linen sheet, and brought me refreshment—fruits, oiled cakes, and a fragrant draught that seemed to both strengthen and stimulate me. Then I was led forth again to the chamber in which the two priests awaited me.

They were there, with another priest of the inferior order, who held in his hands a fine linen garment of pure white. The two priests took this, and, as the others drew away the sheet from my form, they together put it upon me. And when they had done so, they joined their hands upon my head, while the other priests knelt down where they stood.

I knew not what all this meant—I was again becoming alarmed. But the bodily refreshment had done much to soothe my soul, and when without further ceremony, they sent me away again with the two inferior priests, with whom I felt a little familiarized, my spirits arose, and my step became light.

They took me to a small room, in which was a long, low divan covered with a linen sheet. There was nothing else in the room, and indeed I felt as if my eyes and brain might well remain without interest for a while; for how much had I not seen since I entered the temple in the morning! How long it seemed since I had let go my mother's hand at the gate!

"Rest in peace," said one of the priests. "Take your fill of sleep, for you will be awakened in the first cool hours of the night!"

And so they left me.

Chapter III

I lay upon my couch, which was soft enough to make it very welcome to my weary limbs, and before long I was buried in profound sleep, notwithstanding the strangeness of my surroundings. The health and faith of youth enabled me to forget all the newness of my position in the temporary luxury of complete rest. Not long afterwards I have entered that cell to gaze upon that couch, and marvel where the peace of mind had flown that had been mine in my ignorant boyhood.

When I awoke it was quite dark, and I started suddenly to a sitting posture, vividly conscious of a human presence in the room. My wits were scattered by my sudden awakening. I thought myself to be at home, and that it was my mother who was silently watching beside me.

"Mother," I cried out, "what is the matter? Why are you here? Are you ill? Are the sheep astray?"

For a moment there was no answer, and my heart began to beat rapidly as I realized in the midst of the blank darkness that I was not at home—that I was indeed in a new place—that I knew not who it might be that thus silently watched in my room. For the first time I longed for my little homely chamber—for the sound of my mother's voice. And, though I think I was a brave lad, and one not given to womanish weakness, I lay down again and wept aloud.

"Bring lights," said a quiet voice; "he is awake."

I heard sounds, and then a strong fragrance crept to my nostrils. Immediately afterwards two young novices entered at the door, bearing silver lamps, which threw a sudden and vivid light into the room. Then I saw—and the sight so startled me that I ceased to weep and, forgot my home-sickness—I saw that my room was quite full of white-robed priests, all standing motionless. No wonder, indeed, that I had been overpowered by the sense of a human presence in my room. I was surrounded by a silent and statuesque crowd of men whose eyes were bent upon the ground, whose hands were crossed upon their breasts. I sank back again upon my couch and covered my face; the lights, the crowd of faces, overpowered me; and I felt strongly disposed, when I had recovered from my astonishment, to begin weeping again from sheer bewilderment of ideas. The fragrance grew stronger and more intense, the room seemed filled with burning incense; and, opening my eyes, I saw that a young priest on each side of me held the vases which contained it. The room, as I have said, was full of priests; but there was an inner circle close about my couch. Upon the faces of these men I gazed with awe. Among them were Agmahd and Kamen and the others shared with them the strange immobility of expression which had affected me so deeply. I glanced from face to face and covered my eyes again trembling. I felt as though walled in by an impenetrable barrier; I was imprisoned, with these men around me, by something infinitely more impassable than stone walls. The silence was broken at last. Agmahd spoke.

"Arise, child," he said, "and come with us." I arose obediently, though truly I would rather have remained alone in my dark chamber than have accompanied this strange and silent crowd. But I had no choice save silent compliance when I encountered the cold, impenetrable blue eyes which Agmahd turned upon me. I arose, and found that when I moved I was enclosed by the same inner circle. Before, behind, and at the side of me they walked, the others moving in orderly fashion outside the centre. We passed down a long corridor until we reached the great entrance door of the temple. It stood open and I felt refreshed as by the face of an old friend by the glimpse I got of the starlit dome without. But the glimpse was brief. We halted just inside the great doors, and some of the priests closed and barred them; we then turned towards the great central corridor which I had observed on my first entrance. I noticed now that, though so spacious and beautiful, no doors opened into it, save one deep arched one right at the end, facing the great temple avenue. I wondered idly where this solitary door would lead.

They brought a little chair, and placed it in the midst of the corridor. On this I was told to sit, facing the door at the far end. I did so, silent and alarmed;—what meant this strange thing? Why was I to sit thus, with the high priests standing around me? What ordeal was before me? But I resolved to be brave, to have no fear. Was not I already clothed in a pure white linen garment? Truly it was not embroidered in gold; but yet it was not stitched with black, like that of the younger priests. It was pure white; and priding myself that this must mean some sort of distinction. I tried to sustain my failing courage by this idea.

The incense grew so strong that it made my head confused. I was unaccustomed to the scents which the priests so lavishly scattered.

Suddenly—without word or any sign of preparation—the lights were extinguished, and I found myself once more in the dark, surrounded by a strange and silent crowd.

I tried to collect myself and realize where I was. I remembered that the mass of the crowd was behind me, that in front of me the priests had parted, so that, though the inner circle still separated me from the others, I was looking, when the lights were put out, straight down the corridor towards the deep-arched door way.

I was alarmed and miserable. I curled myself together on my seat, intending to be brave, if need be, but in the meantime to remain as silent and unobtrusive as possible. Much did I check the calm faces of those high priests whom I knew to be standing immovably beside me. The absolute silence of the crowd behind filled me with terror and awe. I was at some moments so full of alarm that I wondered whether, if I arose and moved straight down the corridor, I could escape from between the priests unnoticed. But I dared not try it; and indeed the incense combined with the effects of the subtle drink and the quiet were producing an unaccustomed drowsiness.

My eyes were half closed, and I think I might soon have fallen asleep, but my curiosity was suddenly aroused by perceiving that a line of light showed around the edges of the doorway at the far end of the corridor. I opened my eyes wide to look, and soon saw that slowly, very slowly, the door was being opened. At last it stood half-way open and a dim suffused kind of light came forth from it. But at our end of the corridor the darkness remained total and unrelieved, and I heard no sound or sign of life, save a low, subdued breathing from the men who surrounded me.

I closed my eyes after a few moments; for I was gazing so intently out of the darkness that my eyes grew wearied. When I opened them again I saw that there stood a figure just outside the doorway. Its outline was distinct, but the form and face were dim, by reason of the light being behind; yet, unreasonable as it was, I was filled with a sudden horror—my flesh creeped, and I had to use a kind of physical repressive force in order to prevent myself from screaming aloud. This intolerable sense of fear momently increased; for the figure advanced towards me, slowly, and with a kind of gliding motion that was unearthly. I saw now, as it neared, that it was robed in some kind of dark garment, which almost entirely veiled form and face. But I could not see very clearly, for the light from the doorway only faintly reached out from it. But my agony of fear was suddenly augmented by observing that, when the gliding figure nearly approached me, it kindled some kind of light which it held, and which illumined its dim drapery. But this light made nothing else visible. By a gigantic effort I removed my fascinated gaze from the mysterious figure, and turned my head, hoping to see the forms of the priests beside me. But their forms were not to be seen—all was a total blank of darkness. This released the spell of horror that was on me, and I cried out—a cry of agony and fear—and bowed my head in my hands.

The voice of Agmahd fell upon my ear. "Fear not, my child," he said in his melodious, undisturbed accents.

I made an effort to control myself, helped by this sound which savoured at least of something less unfamiliar and terrible than the veiled figure which stood before me. It was there—not close, but close enough to fill my soul with a kind of unearthly terror.

"Speak, child," said again the voice of Agmahd, "and tell us what alarms thee?"

I dared not disobey, though my tongue clove to the roof of my mouth; and, indeed, a new surprise enabled me to speak more easily than otherwise I could have done.

"What," I exclaimed, "do you not see the light from the doorway, and the veiled figure? Oh! send it away; it frightens me!"

A low, subdued murmur seemed to come from all the crowd at once evidently my words excited them. Then the calm voice of Agmahd again spoke:—

"Our queen is welcome, and we do her all reverence."

The veiled figure bowed its head, and then advanced nearer. Agmahd spoke once more, after a pause of total silence—

"Cannot our lady make her subjects more open-eyed, and give them commands as before?"

The figure stooped, and seemed to trace something on the ground. I looked and saw the words in letters of fire, which vanished as they came—

"Yes; but the child must enter my sanctuary alone with me."

I saw the words, I say, and my very flesh trembled with horror. The unintelligible dread of this veiled form was so powerful that I would rather have died than fulfill such a command. The priests were silent, and I guessed that, as the figure, so the fiery letters were invisible to them. Immediately I reflected that if, strange and incredible as it seemed, it were so, they would not know of the command. Terrified as I was, how could I bring myself to frame the words which should bring upon me an ordeal so utterly dreadful?

I remained silent. The figure turned suddenly towards me and seemed to look on me. Then again it traced, in the swiftly vanishing, fiery letters—"Pass on my message."

But I could not; indeed, horror had now made it physically impossible. My tongue was swollen and seemed to fill my mouth.

The figure turned to me with a gesture of fierce anger. With a quick, gliding movement, it darted towards me, and drew the veil from its face.

My eyes seemed to start from their sockets, as that face was upturned close to mine. It was not hideous, though the eyes were full of an icy anger—in anger that flashed not, but froze. It was not hideous, yet it filled me with such loathing and fear as I had never imagined possible, and the horror of it lay in the fearful unnaturalness of the countenance. It seemed to be formed of the elements of flesh and blood, yet it impressed me as being only a mask of humanity—a fearful, corporeal unreality—a thing made up of flesh and blood, without the life of flesh and blood. Into a second were crowded these horrors. Then with a piercing shriek I swooned for the second time in that day— my first day in the temple.

Chapter IV

When I awoke I felt my body to be covered with a cold dew, and my limbs seemed lifeless. I lay helplessly wondering where I was.

It was still and dark, and at best the sense of solitary quiet was delightful. But soon my mind began to review the events which had made the past day seem like a year to me. The vision of the white Lotus-flower grew strong in my eyes, but waned as my terrified soul flew on to the recollection of that later and most horrible sight—that which, indeed, had been the last before them, until now when I awoke in the darkness.

Again I saw it: again, in my imagination, I saw that uplifted face—its ghastly unreality, the cold glare of its cruel eyes. I was unstrung, unnerved, exhausted—and again though now the vision seemed but my own imagination I cried aloud in terror.

Immediately I saw a light approach the doorway of the room, and a priest entered, carrying a silver lamp.

I saw by its rays, that I was in a chamber which I had not before entered. It seemed full of comfort. I saw that soft falling curtains made it secluded, and I felt that the air was full of a pleasant fragrance.

The priest approached, and as he neared me he bowed his head.

"What needs my lord?" he said. "Shall I bring fresh water if thou art thirsty!"

"I am not thirsty," I answered; "I am afraid—afraid of the horrible thing which I have seen."

"Nay," he answered, "it is but thy youth that makes thee afraid. The gaze of our all-powerful lady is at all times enough to make a man swoon. Fear not, for thou art honoured in that thine eyes have vision. What shall I bring to give thee ease?"

"Is it night?" I said, restlessly turning upon my soft couch.

"It is near morning now," answered the priest. "Oh that the day would come!" I exclaimed; "that the blessed sun should blot from my eyes the thing that makes me shudder! I am afraid of the darkness, for the darkness is the evil face!"

"I will stay beside your bed," said the priest quietly. He placed the silver lamp upon a stand and sat down near me. His face relapsed into instant composure, and ere he had been there a moment he seemed to me naught but a carven statue. His eyes were cold: his speech, though full of kind words, had no warmth in it. I shrank away from him; for as I looked on him the vision of the corridor seemed to rise between us. I bore this a while, trying to find comfort in his presence; but at length I burst forth in words, forgetting my fear of giving offence, which had kept me until now so obediently quiet.

"Oh, I cannot bear it!" I cried. "Let me go away; let me go out—into the garden—anywhere! The whole place is full of the vision. I see it everywhere. I cannot shut my eyes against it! Oh, let me—let me go away!"

"Rebel not against the vision" answered the priest. "It came to thee from the sanctuary—from the most sacred shrine. It has marked thee as one different from others, one who will be honoured and eared for among us. But thou must subdue the rebellion of thy heart."

I was silent. The words sank like cold icicles upon my soul. I did not grasp their meaning—indeed, it was impossible that I should; but was sensitively alive to the chill of the speech. After a long pause, in which I tried hard to put thought out of my mind, and so obtain release from my fears, a sudden recollection seized me with an agreeable sense of relief.

"Where," I said, "is the black man whom I saw in the garden yesterday?"

"What?—the gardener, Seboua! He will be sleeping in his chamber. But when the days breaks he rise and go out into the garden."

"May I go with him?" I asked, with feverish anxiety, even clasping my hands as in prayer, so distressed was I lest I should be refused.

"Into the garden? If you are restless, it will soothe the fever that is upon your frame, to go among the morning dews and the fresh flowers. I will call Seboua to fetch you, when I see the dawn breaking."

I heaved a deep sigh of relief at this easy assent to my prayer; and turning away from the priest, lay still with closed eyes, trying to keep all horrid sights or imaginings from me by the thought of the sense of delight which would soon be mine when I should leave the close, artificially perfumed chamber for the sweetness and free inbreathing of the outer air.

I said no word, waiting patiently; and the priest sat motionless beside me. At last, after what seemed to me hours of weary waiting, he arose and extinguished the silver lamp. I saw then that a dim gray light entered the room from the lofty windows.

"I will call Seboua," he said, turning to me, "and send him to you. Remember that this is your chamber, which is henceforth to belong to you. Return here before the morning ceremonies; there will be novices waiting with the bath and oil for your anointment."

"And how," said I, much terrified at the idea of being, by some strange destiny, so important a person—"how shall I know when to return here?"

"You need not come till after the morning meal. A bell rings for that; and, moreover, Seboua will tell you." With these words he departed.

I was full of pleasure at the thought of the fresh air which would revive my unnaturally wearied body; and I longed to see Seboua's strange face, and the sweet smile which would now and then obliterate his ugliness. It seemed as though his had been the only human face I had seen since I parted with my mother.

I looked to see if I still wore my linen garment so that I was ready to go with him. Yes, it was on me, my pure white dress. I looked on it with a sense of pride, for I had never worn anything so finely woven before. I was so far restored to quietude by the idea of being again with Seboua that I lay looking idly at my dress, and wondering what my mother would have thought, seeing me clad in this fine and delicate linen.

It was not long before I heard a step which roused me from my dreaming; Seboua's strange visage appeared in the doorway; Seboua's black form advanced towards me. He was ugly—yes; uncouth—yes; black and without any fairness of appearance. Yet as he entered and looked on me, the smile which I remembered again irradiated his face. He was human!—loving!

I stretched out my hands to him as I rose from my couch.

"O Seboua!" I said, the tears rising in my foolish boy's eyes as I saw this gentleness upon his face—"Seboua, why am I here? What is it that makes them say I am different from others? Seboua, tell me, am I again to see that awful form?"

Seboua came and knelt beside me. It seemed natural in this black man to kneel down when a sense of awe overcame him.

"My son" he said, "thou art gifted from heaven with unclosed eyes. Be brave in the possession of the gift and thou shalt be a light in the midst of the darkness that is descending upon our unhappy land."

"I don't want to be," I said fretfully. I was not afraid of him, and my rebellion must out. "I don't want to do anything which makes one feel so strange. Why have I beheld this ghastly face which even now comes before my eyes and blots out from them the light of day?"

"Come with me," said Seboua, rising instead of answering my question and holding out his hand to me. "Come, and we will go among the flowers, and talk of these things when the fresh airs have cooled thy brow."

I rose, nothing loth, and hand in hand we passed through the corridors until we reached a door that admitted us to the garden.

How can I describe the sense of exhilaration with which I drank in the morning air? It was incomparably greater and keener a delight than anything in the world of nature had ever before imparted to me. Not only did I pass out of a secluded and scented atmosphere, different from any to which I had been accustomed, but also the terrified, over-excited mental state which I was in was infinitely cooled and re-assured by the renewed sense that the world was still beautiful and natural outside the temple doors.

Seboua, looking in my face, seemed by some subtle sympathy to detect my vague thoughts and interpret them to me.

"The sun still rises in all his magnificence," he said. "The flowers still open their hearts to his greeting. Open thou thine, and be content."

I did not answer him. I was young and untaught. I could not readily answer him in words, but I looked up in his face as we moved across the garden and I suppose my eyes must have spoken for me.

"My son" he said, "because in the night you have been into the darkness, there is no reason to doubt that the light still is behind the darkness. You do not fear when lying down to sleep at night that you will see the sun in the morning. You have been into deeper darkness than that of the night, and you will see a brighter sun than this."

I did not understand him, though I revolved his words in my mind. I said nothing, for the sweet air, and the sense of human sympathy, were enough for me. I seemed careless of hearing words, or understanding my experiences, now that I was out in the fresh air. I was but a boy, and the sheer delight of my reviving strength made me forget all else.

This was natural; and all that was natural seemed to me, to-day, to be abundantly full of charm. Yet no sooner had I entered the natural once more and begun to revel in my return to it, than suddenly and unawares I was taken out of it.

Whither? Alas! how can I tell? There are no adequate words in the languages of the world to describe any real thing which lies outside the circle that is called natural.

Surely I stood with my own feet upon the green grass—surely I had not departed from the spot whereon I stood? Surely Seboua stood by me? I pressed his hand. Yes, it was there. Yet I knew by my sensations that the natural had yielded me up, and that again I was within the world of feeling—sight—sound which I dreaded.

I saw nothing—I heard nothing—yet I stood in horror, trembling as the leaves tremble before a storm. What was I about to see? What was near me! What was it that drew a cloud across my eyes?

I closed them. I dared not look. I dared not face the dimness of the realities around me.

"Open thine eyes, my son" said Seboua, "and tell me, is our lady there?"

I opened them, dreading to behold the awful face which had filled me with fear in the darkness of the night. But no—for a moment I saw nothing—and I sighed with relief, for I always expected to see that face uplifted close to mine, with a grin of anger upon it. But in another second my frame thrilled with delight. Seboua had brought me, without my perceiving it, close beside the lotus tank; and I saw, stooping as before, to drink the clear flowing water, the fair woman whose long golden hair half hid her face from me.

"Speak to her!" cried Seboua. "I see by thy face that she is before thee. Oh, speak to her! Not in this generation has she spoken with her priests—speak to her, for indeed we need her help!"

Seboua had fallen on his knees by my side, as yesterday he had done. His face was full of earnestness and glow—his eyes full of a prayer. Looking into them I sank back overcome, I could not tell by what, but it seemed as though the golden-haired woman called me to her, and as though Seboua pushed me towards her, yet in my body I was no nearer to her; but in my consciousness I appeared to rise and move towards the lily tank, until, leaning upon its ledge, I touched her garment where it fell upon the surface of the water. I looked up into her face, but I could not see it. Light radiated from it, and I could only look at it as I might look upon the sun. Yet I felt the touch of her hand upon my head, and words crept into my mind which emanated from her, though I was scarcely conscious that I heard them.

"Child with the open eyes," she said, "thy soul is pure, and upon it is laid a heavy task. But keep thou near to me who am full of light, and I will show thee the way to plant thy feet."

"Mother," said I, "what of the darkness?"

I scarce dared frame my question more plainly. It seemed that if I spoke of that terrible face it would appear in anger before me. I felt a thrill pass through me from her hands as I uttered the words. I fancied that it must be anger which was about to descend on me, but her voice passed into my consciousness as sweetly and softly as raindrops, and imparted to me the same sense of divine sending that we dwellers in a thirsty land associate with the advent of the sweet moisture.

"The darkness is not to be feared; it is to be conquered and driven back, as the soul grows stronger in the light. My son, there is darkness in that innermost sanctuary of the temple, because the worshippers therein cannot bear the light. The light of your world is excluded from it, that it may be illumined with the light of the spirit. But the blind priests, hid in their own conceit, comfort themselves with the brood of darkness. They mock my name by using it; tell them, my son that their queen holds no sway in the realms of darkness. They have no queen; they have no guide but their blind desires. This is the first message you are charged with—did they not ask for one?"

At this moment I seemed drawn back from her. I clung to her garment hem, but my hands were powerless; as I lost my hold upon her I seemed also to lose the sense of her presence. I was conscious only of an intolerable feeling of physical irritation. My eyes had closed, helplessly, as I drew from her; I opened them with an effort. I saw before me only the lotus tank, filled with blossoms of the queen of flowers—filled with blossoms which floated royally upon the surface of the water. The sunshine lay upon their golden hearts, and I saw in them the colour of golden hair. But a voice, full of wrath, though speaking slowly and with deliberate intonation aroused me from dwelling upon the fringe of my dream.

I turned my head and beheld, to my amazement, Seboua standing between two novices; his head bowed, his hands crossed. Near to me stood the high priests Agmahd and Kamen; Agmahd was speaking to Seboua. I soon gathered that he was in disgrace on account of me, but I could not discover what he had done.

Agmahd and Kamen placed themselves on either side of me. And I understood that I was to walk between them. We advanced in silence towards the temple, and entered again its gloomy gates.

Chapter V

I was led into the hall where the priests had been taking their morning meal. The room was almost deserted now; but Agmahd and Kamen remained talking, in their low subdued tones, by one of the windows, while two novices led me to a place by the table, and brought me oiled cakes, fruit, and milk. It was strange to me to be waited on by these youths, who did not speak to me, and whom I regarded with awe as being more experienced than myself in the terrible mysteries of the temple. I wondered, as I ate my cakes, why they had not spoken to me, any of the novices whom I had seen; but looking back over the brief time which I had spent in the temple, I recollected that I had never been left alone with one of them. Even now, Agmahd and Kamen remained in the room, so that, as I saw the silence of fear was upon the faces of the youths who served me. And I fancied it to be a fear, not as of a schoolmaster who uses his eyes like ordinary mortals, but as of some many-sighted and magical observer who is not to be deceived. I saw no gleam of expression on the countenance of either of the youths. They acted like automata.

The exhaustion which had again taken possession of my frame was lessened by the food, and when I had eaten I rose eagerly to look from the high window, to see if Seboua were in the garden. But Agmahd advanced, stepped between me and the window, and gazed upon me with the immovable look which made me dread him so deeply.

"Come," he said. He turned and moved away; I followed him with drooping head, and all my new energy and hope departed; why, I knew not; I could not tell why I gazed upon the embroidered hem of the white garment—which seemed to glide so smoothly over the ground in front of me—with a sense that I was following my doom.

My doom! Agmahd the typical priest of the temple, the real leader among the high priests. My doom.

We passed down the corridors till we entered upon the wide one which led from the gate of the temple to the holy of holies. A horror filled me at the sight of it, even with the sunlight streaming through the gateway, and making mock of its unutterable shadows. Yet so deep was my dread of Agmahd, that, left thus alone with him, I followed him in perfect obedience and silence. We passed down the corridor—with each reluctant step of mine I drew nearer to that terrible door whence, in the darkness of the night, I had seen the hideous form emerge. I was scanning the wall with the kind of terror with which a tormented soul might gaze upon the awful instruments of spiritual inquisition. It is impossible, once looking upon some impending doom with open eyes, not to remain gazing thereon with object yet riveted attention. Such did I in my blind fear bestow upon the walls of the long corridor, which, to my fancy, as we moved down it, seemed to close upon us and to shut us from all the bright, beautiful world which I had lived in until now.

Scanning thus intently these smooth and terrible walls, I perceived, as we approached it, a little door, which stood at right angles with the door of the sanctuary. It would have escaped any observation but one unnaturally tense; for the darkness at this far end of the corridor was deep indeed, by contrast with the glowing sunlight we had left at the other.

We approached this door. As I have said, it stood at right angles with the wall of the sanctuary. It was close to the door of it, but it was in the wall of the corridor.

My steps seemed to be taken without my own volition now; certainly my will would have carried me back to the sunshine which made the world, beautiful with flowers— which made life seem a glorious reality, and not a hideous and unimaginable dream!

Yet there it was—the door—and Agmahd stood, his hand upon it. He turned and looked at me.

"Have no fear," he said, in his calm, equable tones. "Our sanctuary is the centre of our home, and its near neighbourhood is enough to fill us with strength."

I passed through the same experience as when first Agmahd encouraged me by his voice in the garden. I raised my eyes, with an effort, to his, that I might discover whether there was the same encouragement in his beautiful countenance. But all that I saw was the intolerable calm of those blue eyes; they were pitiless, immovable: my soul, aghast, beheld in them at that moment fully the cruelty of the beast of prey.

He turned from me and opened the door; and, passing through it, held it open that I might follow him. I followed him—yes, though my steps seemed to recoil upon myself and lead me to the deeps.

We entered a low-roofed room, lighted by one broad window, high in the wall. It was curtained and draped with rich material; a low couch stood at one side of the room. When my glance fell on the couch I started; why, I know not; but I at once thought it to be the couch which I had slept on in the last night. I could look at nothing else, though there were many beautiful things to look at, for the room was adorned luxuriously. I only wondered, with a shrinking heart, why that couch had been removed from the room in which I had slept.

While I looked on it, lost in conjecture, I suddenly became conscious of silence—complete silence—and of loneliness.

I turned with a sudden alarm.

Yes! I was alone. He was gone—the dread priest Agmahd—he had gone without another word, and let me in this room.

What could it mean? I crossed to the door and tried it. It was fast closed and barred.

I was a prisoner. But what could it mean? I looked around the massive stone walls—I glanced up at the high window—I thought of the near neighbourhood of the sanctuary—and I flung myself upon the couch and hid my face.

I imagine that I must have lain there for hours. I did not dare to arise and make any disturbance. I had nothing to appeal to but the blue, pitiless eyes of the priest Agmahd. I lay upon my couch with fast-closed eyes, not daring to face the aspect of my prison and praying that the night might never come.

It was yet the early part of the day, that I felt sure of, although I knew not how long a time I had passed in the garden with Seboua. The sun was high, and streamed in at my window. I saw this as, after a long time had passed, I turned and looked around, my room with a sudden and alarmed glance. I had the idea that some one was in it—but, unless hidden behind the curtains, no visible form was in the room.

No, I was alone. And as I gathered courage to look up to the sunlight that made my window a thing glorious for the eyes, I began to realize that it still veritably was in existence; and that, notwithstanding my recent hideous experiences, I was nothing but a boy who loved sunshine.

The attraction grew very strong, and at last fanned itself into the wish to climb up to the high window and look. The passion which caused me to desire so ardently to do this, having once thought of it, I can no more account for than I could for most of the inquisitive and headstrong purposes of a boy's brain. At all events I rose from my couch—casting all terror of my surroundings to the winds, now that I had a purpose sufficiently childish to absorb me. The wall was perfectly smooth; but I fancied that, by standing on a table that was beneath the window, I could reach the sill with my hands, and so raise myself up to see out. I soon climbed the table, but I could barely reach the sill with upstretched arms. I jumped a little, and just catching hold of the sill managed to draw myself upwards. I suppose that part of the enterprise must have been the delight to me; for I certainly did not anticipate seeing anything but the temple gardens.

What I saw, though there was nothing perhaps very startling, sobered my enjoyment.

The gardens were not there. My window looked out upon a small square piece of ground, which was surrounded by high blank walls. I soon saw that these were evidently walls of the temple, not outer walls. The piece of ground was enclosed in the very heart of the great building, for I could see its columns and roofs rising beyond each side, and the walls were blank. Mine was the only window I could perceive any trace of.

At that moment I heard a faint sound in the room, and, quickly letting myself drop, I stood upon the table, looking round in consternation. The sound seemed to proceed, from behind a heavy curtain that half covered one wall. I stood breathless, and, even in this broad daylight and gleaming sunshine, somewhat in terror of what I might see.

For I had no idea that there was any mode of entrance but that door by which I had come, so that I scarce dared to hope for a wholesome human presence!

These fears soon vanished, however, for the curtain was drawn a little back, and a black-robed novice—whom I had not seen before—crept from out its shelter. I wondered at his stealthy manner; but I had no fears, for he held in his hand a glorious blossom of the royal white lotus flower. I sprang from the table and advanced towards him, my eyes upon the flower. When quite close he spoke, very low and quickly.

"This," he said, "is from Seboua. Cherish it, but let none of the priests see it. Cherish it, and it will help you in hours when you will need help; and Seboua urges that you remember all the words he has said to you, and that you trust, above all, to your love for the truly beautiful and to your natural likes and dislikes. That is the message," he said, stepping back towards the curtain. "I am risking my life here to please Seboua. Be careful that you never come near this door, or show that you know it exists; it opens into the private room of the high priest Agmahd, into which none dare enter save on peril of intolerable punishment."

"And how have you come through?" I asked in great curiosity.

"They are engaged in the morning ceremonies—all the priests—and I succeeded in escaping unseen to come to you."

"Tell me," I cried, holding him even as he endeavoured to hurry through the door, "why did not Seboua come?"

"He cannot—he is closely watched that he may make no effort to get near you."

"But why is this?" I exclaimed in dismay and wonder.

"I cannot tell," said the novice, extracting his garment from my grasp. "Remember the words I have said."

He hastily passed through the door and closed it behind him. I found myself half smothered by the heavy curtain and, as soon as I could recover from my amazement at this sudden appearance and disappearance, I moved it aside and stepped out, the lily in my hand.

My first thought, even before I would let myself think over the words which I was to remember—was to place my precious flower in some safe place. I held it tenderly, as though it were the breathing form of one I loved. I looked around anxiously, wondering where it would be both unseen and yet preserved.

I saw, after a few moments spent in hasty inspection that just behind the head of my couch there was a corner which the curtain fell a little away from. Here, at least, I might place it for a while; it would have room to breathe, and would not be seen unless the curtain were moved away— and behind my couch seemed a less likely place for it to be discovered in than any other. I hastily placed it here, afraid to keep it in my hand lest the ceremonies should be over and Agmahd enter my room. So I hid it, and then looked around for some vessel of water in which I might place it, for it occurred to me that, if I did not supply it with some of that element which it so dearly loved, it would not live long to be my friend.

I found a little earthen jar of water and placed it in it, wondering the while what I should do if the priests, discovering its absence, should ask me for it. I could not tell what to do in such an emergency; but, if the flower were discovered, I could only hope that some inspiration would be given me by which I might avoid throwing further blame upon Seboua; for, though I could not understand why or how, it was very evident that he had been blamed for something in connection with me.

I went and sat on the couch, to be near my beloved flower. How I desired that I might place it in the sunshine and revel in its beauties!

In this way the day passed. No one came near me. I watched the sun pass away from my window. I watched the shadows of evening descend upon it. I was still alone. I do not think I grew more terrified. I do not remember that the coming night brought with it any agony of fear. I was filled with a deep calmness, which either the long undisturbed hours of the day had produced, or else it was wrought by the beautiful though unseen flower; for that was ever before my eyes in all its radiant and delicate beauty. I had none of the intolerable visions which I had been unable to drive from me in the former night.

It was quite dark when the door which communicated with the corridor opened, and Agmahd entered, followed by a young priest, who brought me food and a cup of some strange sweet-smelling syrup. I should not have stirred from my couch had it not been that I longed for food. I had not thought of it before, but I was indeed faint and fasting. I rose eagerly, therefore, and, when the young priest brought the food to my side, I drank first of the syrup—which indeed he offered me first—for my exhaustion suddenly became plain to me.

Agmahd looked on me as I drank. When I had put down the cup, I raised my eyes to his with a new defiance.

"I shall go mad," I said boldly, "if you leave me in this room alone. I have never been left alone so long in all my life."

I spoke under a sudden impulse. When I had been passing the long hours in solitude they had not seemed so terrible; but now, with a quick apprehension of the evil of this solitariness, I spoke out my feeling.

Agmahd said to the young priest—

"Set the food down and fetch hither the book that lies upon the couch in my outer room."

He departed on his errand, Agmahd said nothing to me; and I—having said my say, and not having, as I rather expected, been annihilated for it—took up an oiled cake from the platter, and cheerfully went on with my meal.

Five years after I could not have faced Agmahd in this way. I could not have eaten my all having just defied him. But now I was elated by the supreme ignorance and indifference of youth. I had no measuring line for the depths of the priest's intellect—the wide embracingness of his stern cruelty. How should I have? I was ignorant. And, moreover, I had no clue to the mode of his cruelty—the purpose, the intention of it. I was in the dark altogether. But I was well aware that my life in the temple was not what I had looked for if it was to be like this, and I already cherished boyish notions of escaping from it (even down the terrible corridor) if I were to exist after such an unhappy fashion. I little knew when I thought of this how well I was guarded.

Agmahd said no word while I ate and drank, and presently the young priest opened the door and entered, bearing in his hands a large black book. He placed it on a table which Agmahd told him to draw near to my couch. A lamp was then brought by him from a corner of the room and placed on the table. He lighted it, and this done, Agmahd spoke:

"You need not be lonely if you look within those pages."

So saying, he turned and left the room, followed by the young priest.

I opened it at once. It seems, looking back on that time, that I was to the full as inquisitive as most boys; at all events, any new object riveted my attention for the time being. I opened the black covers of the volume and gazed on the first page. It was beautifully coloured, and I looked in pleasure at the colours a little while before I began to spell out the letters. They stood out from a gray background in letters of so brilliant a hue that they seemed like fire. The title was—"The Arts and Powers of Magic."

It was nonsense to me. I was a comparatively uneducated boy, and I wondered what companionship Agmahd supposed such a book could afford me.

I turned idly over its pages. They were all unintelligible to me, by very reason even of the words used, apart from the matter. The thing was ridiculous, to have sent me this book to read. I yawned widely over it, and closing the book was about to lie down again upon my couch, when I was startled to observe that I was not alone. On the other side of the little table whereon my book and lamp were, stood a man in a black dress. He was looking earnestly upon me, but when I returned his gaze he seemed to retreat from me a little. I wondered how he could have entered so noiselessly and approached so near me without sound.

Chapter VI

"Have you any wish?" said the man in a clear, but very low voice.

I looked at him in surprise. He was a novice, it seemed, by his dress; yet he spoke as though he could gratify my wish—and that, too, without the tone of a mere servant.

"I have just taken food," I answered. "I have no wish—but for freedom from this room."

"That," he answered quietly, "is soon gratified. Follow me."

I stared in astonishment. This novice must know my position—must know of Agmahd's will with regard to me. Dare be thus defy him?

"No," I answered; "the high priests have imprisoned me here; if I am found escaping I shall be punished!"

"Come!" was all his answer. And as he spoke he raised one hand commandingly. As in physical pain I cried aloud; why, I could not realize. Yet my sense seemed to be that I was held as by a vice—that some intolerable power grasped my frame and shook it. A second after I stood beside my mysterious visitor, my hand tight clasped in his. "Look not back!" he cried. "Come with me."

And I followed him. Yet, at the door I desired to turn my head to look; and by what seemed a great effort, I did so.

Little marvel that he bade me not look back! Little marvel that he strove to hurry me from the room, for when my eyes had once turned I remained spellbound, gazing—resisting his iron grasp.

I saw myself—or rather my unconscious form—and then for the first time, I understood that my companion was no denizen of earth—that I had again entered the land of shadows.

But this wonder was wholly swallowed up in a larger one—one sufficient to make me strong against the effort of my companion to draw me from the room.

Leaning over the couch—standing behind it and bending forward, in that delicious drooping attitude in which I had first seen her when she stooped to drink the water—I saw the Lily Queen.

And I heard her speak. Her voice came to me like the dropping of water—like the spray of a fountain.

"Wake, sleeper—dream no more, nor remain within this accursed spell."

"Lady, I obey," I murmured, within myself, and instantly a mist seemed to enwrap me. I was but dimly conscious—yet I knew that, in obedience to the wish of the beautiful queen I was endeavouring to return to my natural state. I succeeded by degrees, and opened my eyes wearily and heavily, to behold a desolate empty room. The novice had left me—of that I was glad—but, alas! the Lady of the Lotus had left me also. The room seemed empty indeed, and my heart was heavy as I looked around me. I felt the sweet Lady of the Flower more as a beautiful mother in my childish heart, than as a queen. I yearned for her soft presence. But it was not there. I knew only too well that she was not in the room hidden from me. I felt her absence with my soul as well as perceived it with my eyes.

I raised myself languidly enough, for, indeed, this last struggle had out-wearied me, and went to the corner behind my couch where my dear flower was hid. I drew back the curtain a little way, to look at my treasure. Alas! it was already drooping its lovely head! I sprang forward to assure myself that I had indeed given it water. Yes, its stem was deeply plunged in its lower element. Yet the flower drooped like a dead thing, and the stem bent inertly over the edge of the vessel.

"My flower," I cried, kneeling down beside it, "art thou too gone?—am I quite alone?"

I took the languid flower-form from the vessel and placed it upon my breast, within my robe. And then wholly disconsolate for the moment, I flung myself again upon my couch and closed my eyes, endeavouring to make them dark and visionless.

How?—who knows the way to hide visions from the inner eye, that eye which has the terrible gift of sight which no darkness can blind? I did not, then at all events.

The night had descended on the earth, when I aroused myself from my long and silent rest. It was moonlight without, and a silvery streak of light entered at the high window and streamed into my room. Within that streak of light came the hem of a white garment; a hem gold-embroidered. I knew the embroidery—I raised my eyes slowly, for I expected to recognize Agmahd, as indeed I did. He stood just within the dim shadow; but his bearing was not easily confused with that of another man even if his face were unseen.

I lay perfectly still; yet he seemed immediately to know that I was awake.

"Rise," he said. I rose, and stood beside my couch, with wide eyes of fear fixed upon him.

"Drink that which is beside you," he said. I looked and saw a cup full of red liquid. I drank it, blindly hoping it might give me strength to bear whatever ordeal the silent hours of this night might be destined to bring upon me.

"Come," he said; and I followed him to the door. I half unconsciously cast a glance up to the window, in the thought that perchance fresh air and freedom lay before me. Suddenly I felt myself blinded—quickly I put my hand to my eyes; a soft substance was bound over them. I was silent with the silence of wonder and of fear; I felt myself supported and led onward carefully. I shuddered as I thought that it must be the arm of Agmahd which upheld me, but I submitted to the contact, knowing that I was powerless to resist it.

We moved onwards slowly; I was conscious of leaving my own room and of traversing some distance beyond it, but how far or in what direction I was unable to guess, bewildered as I was by my blindfold state.

We paused in utter silence; the arm around me was removed, and I felt the bandage taken from my eyes. They opened upon a darkness so complete that I raised my hand to assure myself that the kerchief was not still upon them. No—they were free—they were open—yet they gazed upon nothing but a blank wall of deep and total darkness. My head was full of pain and dizziness—the fumes of the strong syrup that I had drunk seemed to have filled it with confusion. I remained motionless, hoping to recover myself and realize my position.

While I waited, I suddenly became conscious of a new presence close beside me. I did not shrink from it. I seemed to know it to be beautiful, to be friendly and glorious. I was thrilled with a yearning, an indescribable sense of leaning in spirit towards the unknown presence.

Amid the silence suddenly came low, sweet speech close to mine ear.

"Tell Agmahd that he disobeys the law. One priest alone may enter the holy of holies, and no more."

I recognized the liquid water-like voice of the Lily Queen. Although I was unaware of the priest's presence I unhesitatingly obeyed my queen.

"One priest alone may enter the holy of holies," I said, "and no more. Agmahd being here the law is disobeyed."

"I demand to hear the utterance of the queen" came the reply in the solemn tones of Agmahd.

"Tell him," said that other voice which thrilled my soul and made my frame vibrate, "that had I been able to reveal myself in his presence I had not waited for you."

I repeated her words. There was no answer, but I heard a movement—footsteps—and a door closed softly. Immediately a soft hand touched me. I was simultaneously conscious of the touch, and of a faint light upon my chest. I felt in a second that the hand was put within my dress to draw forth the withered lily which I had hid there. But I did not attempt to hinder this, for, looking up as a light attracted my eyes, I beheld standing before me the Lily Queen. My queen as in my boyish heart I had begun to call her, I saw dimly and as enveloped in a shadowy mist, but yet plainly enough to make me rejoice in her near presence. And as I looked I saw that she held close to her bosom the withered flower which she had taken from mine. And I saw, wonderingly, that it faded yet more, grew dimmer, and wholly vanished. Yet I did not regret it, for, as it died away, she grew more bright and distinct to my sight. When the flower had wholly disappeared she stood beside me, clear and distinct, illuminated by her own radiance.

"Fear no longer," she said, "they cannot harm thee, for thou hast entered within my atmosphere. And though they have placed thee in the very dungeon of vice and falsehood, have no fear, but observe all things, and remember what thine eyes perceive."

The darkness appeared to become illumined by her confident and gracious words. I grew bold, and full of strength.

She held out her hand and touched me gently. The touch filled me with a fire that excelled any warmth I had ever experienced.

"The royal flower of Egypt dwells upon the sacred waters, which in their purity and peace fitly form its eternal resting-place. I am the spirit of the flower; I am sustained upon the waters of truth, and my life is formed of the breath of the heavens, which is love. But the degradation of my earthly resting-place, over which my wings of love yet brood, is driving from it the light of heaven which is wisdom. Not long can the spirit of the royal lotus live in darkness; the flower droops and dies if the sun be withdrawn from it. Remember these words, child, grave them upon your heart, for as your mind becomes capable of grasping them, they will enlighten you in many things."

"Tell me," I said, "when may I again visit the lilies? Will you not take me there in to-morrow's sunshine? Now it is night, and I am tired; may I not sleep at your feet, and to-morrow be with you in the garden?"

"Poor child," she said, stooping towards me so that her breath fanned me, and it was sweet like the scent of wild flowers, "how hardly have they taxed thee! Rest here in my arms, for thou art to be my seer, and the enlightener of my loved land. Strength and health must dwell upon thy brow like jewels. I will guard thee; sleep, child."

I lay down at her bidding, and though I knew that I was upon a cold, hard floor, I felt that my head rested upon an arm soft and full of magnetic soothing; and I fell into deep, dreamless, undisturbed slumber.

There was writ in Agmahd's secret volume of records but one word that night—"Vain."

Chapter VII

A white flower was in my hand when I awoke. Its beauty filled my heart with gladness, I looked on it and was refreshed and content, as though I had slept in my mother's arms, and this was her kiss on my lips, for I held the flower, a half-blown lotus-blossom, close to my mouth. I did not wonder at first how I had obtained it, I only looked upon its beauty and was happy, for it made me know that my queen, my one friend, did indeed guard me.

Suddenly I saw some one enter the room, yet she did not so much enter it, as seem to come out of the shadow. I lay, as now I saw, on the couch in the room to which Agmahd had brought me. I was scarcely aware of how, or in what place, I had spent the dark hours of the night, but I felt that it was in his arms I had been carried back to my couch. I was glad to be there again and I was glad to see this child that approached me. She was younger than myself, and bright as the sunshine. She came near to me, and then paused; I put out my hand to her.

"Give me the flower," she said.

I hesitated, for the possession of the flower made me happy, but I could not refuse her, for she smiled, and none within the temple had smiled on me till now. I gave her my blossom.

"Ah!" she cried, "there is water on its leaves!" and she flung it away from her as if in disgust. I started from my couch in angry haste to rescue my treasure. Instantly the child snatched it up again and fled from me with a cry of laughter. I followed her at my utmost speed. I was only a boy, and like a boy I chased her, for I was angry, and determined she should not win. We sped through great rooms wherein we saw no one, the child darting through the great curtains, and I following with the swiftness of a lad of the country. But suddenly I came against what seemed to me a wall of solid stone. How was it she could have eluded me? for I was close on her footsteps. I turned back in a passion of rage that made me blind, but I was silenced and stricken into quiet, for the priest Agmahd stood before me. Had I done wrong? It could not be, for he was smiling.

"Come with me," he said; and spoke so gently that I did not fear to follow him. He opened a door, and I saw before my eyes a garden full of flowers, a square garden enclosed in hedges, thickly covered too with flowers, and this garden was full of children all running hither and thither as swiftly as possible, in the intricacies of some game I did not understand. There were so many, and they moved so swiftly, that at first I was bewildered, but suddenly I saw the child among them who had taken my flower. She wore it on her dress, and she smiled in mockery as she saw me. I plunged into the crowd immediately, and seemed, though I knew not how, at once to obey the laws of the game or dance. I scarce knew which it was, for though I moved rightly among them, I could not tell what object they had in pursuit. I followed, and chased the figure of the girl. Although I did not succeed in approaching her, so swift was she, yet I grew quickly to enjoy the motion, the excitement, the merry faces, and laughing voices. The scent of the innumerable flowers filled me with delight, and I became passionately desirous to possess myself of some of them. I forgot the lotus blossom in thinking of these others, and yet

I hurried on in the maze of the dance, promising myself a great cluster of flowers when the dance ceased; at that moment I did not fear Agmahd or his displeasure, even if this garden were his. Then suddenly I heard a shout of a hundred gay children's voices.

"He has won it! He has won it!"

It was a ball, a golden ball, and light, so light, that I could throw it far, far up in the sky; yet it always return to my uplifted hands. I had found it at my feet when I heard the others shout, and immediately I knew the ball was mine. Now, I saw there was no one near me but the child, who had taken my lotus flower. It was not on her dress now, and I had forgotten it. But she was smiling, and I laughed to see her. I threw her the ball, and she threw it back to me, from one end of the garden to the other.

Suddenly a bell rang out clear and loud in the air. "Come," she said; "it is school-time, come." She caught my hand and threw the ball away. I looked longingly after it.

"That was mine," I said.

"It is no use now," she answered. "You must gain another prize."

We ran away, hand in hand, through another garden into a great room which I had not seen before. The children with whom I had played were here and a great many more. The air was heavy and sweet in this room. I was not tired, for I had but just risen from my long sleep and the morning was yet fresh, but now that I entered this room I felt weary and my head burned.

Very soon I fell asleep, hearing the children's voices round me. When I awoke it was to hear a shout like that in the garden. "He has won it! He has won it!"

I stood upon a kind of throne—a lofty seat of marble. And I could hear my own voice in the air. I had been speaking. The children were round me, but they were clustered upon and about the marble seat. I remembered that the child who brought me here had said the teacher stood upon this throne. Why then were we, the children here? I looked, and lo, I saw that the room was full of priests! They stood in the place of the taught. They stood silent, immovable. Again I heard the children cry, "He has won it! He has won it!" I sprang from the throne in a sudden frenzy, I knew not why. As I stood upon the ground I looked and saw that the children were gone. I could not see any one of them but the child who had brought me here. She was standing on the throne, and she laughed and clapped her hands with glee. I wondered what it was that pleased her, and looking down I saw that I stood in a circle of white robed priests who had prostrated themselves until their foreheads touched the ground. What did this mean? I could not guess, and stood still in terror, when suddenly the child cried out as if in answer to my thought, "They worship you!"

My wonder at her words was not greater than another wonder which fell on me. For I understood that I alone heard her voice.

Chapter VIII

I was taken back to my own room, and there the young priests brought me food. I was hungry, for I had not broken my fast, and I found the food exquisite. The young priests who brought it to me fell on one knee when they offered it; I looked wonderingly at them, for I could not guess why they should do so. Many of them came with fruits and rich syrup and delicate sweetmeats, such as I had never seen, and with flowers. Great clusters of flowers were brought and placed near me, and bushes covered with blossoms were put against the wall. I cried out with pleasure to see them, and as I cried out I saw Agmahd standing within the shadow of the curtain. His eyes were on me, cold odd smiles. Yet I did not fear him now; I was full of a new spirit of pleasure, which made me bold. I went from flower to flower, kissing the blossoms. Their scent filled all the room with its richness. I was glad and proud, for I felt as if I need no longer be afraid of this cold priest, who stood motionless as though cut in marble. This sensation of fearlessness lifted a weight of agony from my childish soul.

He turned and vanished, and as he passed under the curtain I saw the child at my side.

"See," she said, "I brought you these flowers."

"You!" I exclaimed.

"Yes, I told them you loved flowers. And these are strong and sweet; they grow in the earth. Are you tired, or shall we go out and play? Do you know that garden is our own and the ball is there? Some one took it back for you."

"Tell me," I said, "why the priests kneel to me to-day.

"Do you not know?" she said, looking at me curiously. "It is because you taught from the throne today, and spoke wise words they understood, but we could not. But we saw you had won a great prize. You will win all the prizes."

I sat down upon my couch, and held my head with my hands and looked at her in wonder.

"But how could I do that and not know it?" I demanded.

"You will be great when you do not struggle, when you do not know it you will win all the prizes. If you are quiet and happy you will be worshipped by all these priests, even the most splendid."

I was dumb with wonder for a moment, then I said—

"You are very little. How can you know all this?"

"The flowers told me," she said with a laugh. "They are your friends. But it is all true. Now come and play with me."

"Not yet," I said. And indeed I felt my head was hot and heavy, and my heart filled with wonder I could not understand her words.

"It is impossible I can have taught from the throne," I exclaimed.

"You did! and the high priests bowed their awful faces before you. For you told them how to perform some strange ceremony where you would be in the midst."

"I!"

"Yes, for you told them of what should be your dress, and how to prepare it, and what words to utter, as they placed it on you."

I watched her with passionate interest. "Can you tell me more?" I cried, when she ceased.

"You are to live among earth-fed flowers, and to dance with the children often. Oh, there were many things. But of the ceremony I cannot remember. But you will soon see, for it is to be to-night."

I started from my couch in a sudden frenzy of fear.

"Do not be afraid," she said, with a laugh. "For I am to be with you. That makes me glad, for I belong to the temple, yet have I never been admitted to one of the sacred ceremonies."

"You belong to the temple! But they cannot hear your voice!"

"Sometimes they cannot see me!" she said, laughing, "only Agmahd can always see me, for I am his. But I cannot talk to him. I like you because I can talk to you. Come, let us go out and play. The flowers in the garden are as sweet as these, and the ball is there. Come."

She took my hand and went quietly away. I let her lead me, for I was lost in thought. But outside the air was so rich and sweet, the flowers so bright, the sun so warm, that soon I forgot my thoughts in happiness.

Chapter IX

It was night. I was sleepy and content, for I had been happy and amused, running hither and thither in the sweet-scented air. All the evening I had slept on my couch among the flowers that made my room fragrant, and I dreamed strange dreams in which each flower became a laughing face, and my ears were full of the sound of magic voices. I awoke suddenly and fancied I must be still dreaming, for the moonlight came into my room and fell upon the beautiful blossoms. And I thought with wonder of the simple home I had been reared in. How have I ever endured it? For now it I seemed to me that beauty was life.

I was very happy.

As I lay dreamily looking at the moonlight, the door in the corridor was suddenly opened from without. The corridor was full of light, such brilliant light that the moonlight seemed like darkness, and I was blinded. Then a number of neophytes entered my room, bringing with them some things that I could not see, because of the strong light. Then they went away and closed the door, leaving me alone in the moonlight, with two tall, white-robed, motionless forms. I knew who was with me though I dared not look—it was Agmahd and Kamen Baka.

At first I trembled, but suddenly I saw the child glide forth from the shadow, her finger on her lips and a smile on her face.

"Do not be afraid," she said. "They are going to put on you the beautiful robe you told them to prepare."

I rose from my couch and looked at the priests. I was no longer afraid. Agmahd stood motionless, his eyes fixed on me. The other approached me, holding in his hands a white robe. It was of fine linen and covered with rich gold embroidery, which I saw formed characters I could not understood. It was more beautiful than Agmahd's robe and I had never seen anything so beautiful as that when I entered the temple.

I was pleased, and held out my hand for the robe. Kamen came close to me, and when I flung aside the one I wore, put this upon me with his own hands.

It was steeped with a subtle perfume, which I inhaled with delight. This seemed to me a royal robe!

Kamen advanced to the door and opened it. The brilliant light streamed in full upon me. Agmahd remained standing motionless, his eyes fixed on me.

The child looked upon me with admiration and clapped her hands in delight. Then she held out one hand and took mine. "Come," she said. I yielded, and together we went into the corridor, Agmahd close behind us. The scene we entered startled me, and I paused. The great corridor was full of priests, save just where I stood, close to the door of the holy of holies. Here a large space was left, and in this space stood a couch covered with silken drapery, embroidered with gold, in characters resembling those upon my dress. About the couch was a bank or hedge of sweet smelling flowers, and all around the ground was strewn with plucked blossoms. I shrank from the great crowd of motionless white-robed priests, whose eyes were fixed on me, but the beautiful colours pleased me.

"This couch is for us," said the child, and led me to it. No one else spoke or moved, and I obeyed her. We advanced, and upon the couch found our golden ball with which we had played in the garden. I looked in a sudden wonder to see if Agmahd watched us. He stood by the door of the holy of holies; his eyes were on me. Kamen stood nearer to us, and he was gazing at the closed door of the sanctuary, and his lips were moving as if he were repeating words. No one seemed angry with us, so I looked back at the child. She snatched up the ball and sprang to one end of the great couch; I could not resist her gaiety; I sprang to the other end of the couch, and laughed too. She flung me the ball; I caught it in my hands, but before I could throw it back to her, the corridor was plunged into complete profound darkness. For a moment my breath died away in the sudden agony of fear, but suddenly I found that I could see the child, and that she was laughing. I flung her the ball, and she caught it, and laughed again. I looked around, and saw that all else was black darkness. I thought of the awful figure I had seen before in the darkness, and I must have cried aloud with fear but for the child. She came to me and put her hand in mine.

"Are you afraid?" she said; "I am not. And you need not fear. They would not harm you, for they worship you!"

While she spoke, I heard music—gay, wonderful music—that made my heart beat fast and my feet long to dance.

A moment later and I saw the light come round the sanctuary door, and the door open. Was that awful figure coming forth? My limbs shook at the thought, but yet I did not lose all courage as before. The child's presence and the gay music kept from me the horror of solitude. The child rose, holding my hand in hers. We approached the sanctuary door. I was unwilling, yet I could not resist the guidance which led me on. We entered the door, and as we did so the music ceased. All was still again. But there was a faint light within the sanctuary which seemed to come from the far end of the chamber. The child led me towards this light. She was with me, and I was not afraid. At the end of the chamber was a small inner room, or recess, cut, as I could see, in the rock. I could see this, for there was enough light here. A woman sat on a low seat, her head bent over a great book, which she held open on her knee. My eyes were riveted to her instantly, and I could not remove them. I knew her, and the heart within me shuddered at the thought that she would raise her head, and I should see her face.

Suddenly I knew my companion the child, was gone. I did not look to see, for my eyes were held by a supreme fascination, but I felt my hand had no answering clasp. I knew her presence was gone.

I waited, standing still as one of those figures carved in the avenue of the temple.

At last she lifted her head and looked at me. My blood shivered and grew cold. It seemed to myself that I froze, for those eyes cut like steel, yet I could not resist or turn away, or even hide my eyes from that awful sight.

"You have come to me to learn. Well, I will teach you," she said, and her voice sounded low and sweet like the soft tones of a musical instrument. "You love beautiful things and flowers. You will be a great artist if you live for beauty alone, but you must be more than that." She held out her hand to me, and, against my will, I lifted mine, and gave it her but she barely touched it; at the touch my hand was suddenly full of roses, and all the place was filled with their scent. She laughed, and the sound was musical; I suppose my face pleased her.

"Come now," she said, "and stand nearer me, for you no longer fear me." With my eyes upon the roses, I approached her; they held my sight, and I did not fear her when I did not see her face.

She put her arm round me and drew me close to her side. Suddenly I saw that the dark robe she wore was no garment of linen or cloth—it was alive—it was a drapery of coiling snake, who clung about her and made folds that had seemed to me like soft hanging draperies when I stood a little away from her. Now terror overcame me; I tried to scream but could not, I tried to fly from her but could not. She laughed again but this time her laugh was harsh. But while I looked all was changed, and her robe was dark— dark still but not alive. I stood breathless, wondering in cold with fear—her arm was still about me! She raised her other hand and placed it on my forehead. Then fear left me altogether; I seemed happy and quiet. My eyes were shut, although I saw; I was conscious, yet I did not desire to move. She rose, and lifting me in her arms, placed me on the low stone seat where she had herself been sitting. My head fell back against the wall of rock behind me. I was dumb and still, but I could see.

She rose up to her full height and stretched her arms aloft above her head, and again I saw the serpents. They were vigorous and full of life. They were not only her dress but they were about her head. I could not tell if they were her hair or if they were in it. She clasped her hands high above her head, and the terrible creatures hung wreathing from her arms. But I was not afraid. Fear seemed to have left me forever.

Suddenly I became aware that there was another presence in the sanctuary. Agmahd was there, standing at the door of the inner cavern.

I looked in wonder at his face, it was so still; the eyes were unseeing. Then I knew suddenly that they were in very fact unseeing; that this figure, this light, I myself, were all invisible to him.

She turned to me, or leaned towards me, so that I saw her face, and her eyes were on mine; otherwise she did not move. Those eyes that cut like steel no longer filled me with terror, but they held me with a grasp as of some iron instrument. While I watched her, suddenly I saw the serpents change and vanish; they became long sinuous folds of some soft gray gleaming garment, and their hands and terrible eyes changed into starry groups of roses. And a rich strong scent of roses filled the sanctuary. Then I saw Agmahd smile.

"My Queen is here," he said.

"Your Queen is here," I said, and did not know I had spoken till I heard my own voice. "She waits to know your desire."

"Tell me," he said, " what is her robe?" I answered, "It shines and gleams, and on her shoulders are roses."

"I do not desire pleasure," he said; "my soul is sick of it. But I demand power."

Until now her eyes fixed on mine had told me what to speak; but now I heard her voice again.

"In the temple?"

And I repeated her words, unconscious that I did so till I caught the echo of my voice.

"No," answered Agmahd contemptuously. "I must go outside these walls, and mix with men and work my will among them. I demand the power to do this. It was promised to me; that promise has not been fulfilled."

"Because you lacked the courage and the strength to compel its fulfillment."

"I lack those no longer," answered Agmahd, and for the first time I saw his face flame with passion.

"Then utter the fatal words," she said.

Agmahd's face changed. He stood still for some moments, and his face grew colder and more stony than any carven form.

"I renounce my humanity," he said at last, uttering the words slowly, so that they appeared to pause and rest upon the air.

"It is well," she said. "But you cannot stand alone. You must bring me others ready like yourself to brave all and know all. I must have twelve sworn servants. Get me these, and you shall have your desire."

"Are they to be my equals?" demanded Agmahd.

"In desire and in courage, yes; in power, no; because each will have a different desire; thus will their service be acceptable to me."

Agmahd paused a moment. Then he said, "I obey my Queen. But I must be aided in so difficult a task. How shall I tempt them?"

At these words she flung out her arms, opening and shutting her hands with a strange gesture, which I could not understand. Her eyes gleamed like hot coals, and then grew cold and dull.

"I will direct you," she answered. "Be faithful to my orders and you need not fear. Only obey me and you shall succeed. You have every element within this temple. There are ten priests ready to our hand. They are full of hunger. I will satisfy them. You I will satisfy when your courage and steadfastness is proved—not until then for you demand much more than these others."

"And who shall be the one to complete the number?" asked Agmahd.

She turned her eyes again upon me.

"This child," she answered. "He is mine—my chosen and favourite servant. I will teach him: and through him I will teach you."

Chapter X

"Tell Kamen Baka, that I know his heart's desire, and that he shall have it, but that he must first pronounce the fatal words."

Agmahd bowed his head and turned away. He silently left the sanctuary.

I was again alone with her. She approached me and fastened her terrible eyes on mine.

While I gazed at her she vanished from before me, and in her place was a golden light which gradually shaped itself into a form more beautiful than any I had ever seen.

It was a tree full of foliage that hung soft like hair rather than leaves, and on each branch was a multitude of flowers growing in thick clusters, and among the flowers were a number of birds all golden and gay with brilliant colours, and they darted hither and thither among the glowing blossoms, till my eyes grew dazzled, and I cried aloud, "Oh give me one of these little birds for my own that it may come to me and nestle as it does in those flowers."

"You shall have a hundred of them, and they will so love you they will kiss your mouth and take food from your lips. By-and-by you shall have a garden in which a tree like this shall grow, and all the birds of the air will love you. But first you must do my bidding. Speak to Kamen and bid him enter the sanctuary."

"Enter," I said, "the priest Kamen Baka shall enter."

He came and stood within the doorway of the inner cavern. The tree had vanished, and I saw before me the dark figure with its shining flowing robes and cruel eyes; they were fixed on the priest.

"Tell him," she said slowly, "that his heart's hunger shall be satisfied. He desires love—he shall have it. The priests of the temple have turned cold faces towards him, and he feels that their hearts are as stone. He wants to see them on their knees around him, adoring him, willing slaves. He shall have it; for he shall take upon him this once, which until now has been mine. He shall gratify their heart's lust, and in return they will put him alone upon a pedestal above all but myself. Is the bribe great enough?"

She said these words in a tone of intense contempt, and I could read in her terrible face that she despised him for the narrow limit of his ambition. But the sting left the words as I repeated them.

Kamen bowed his head, and a strange glow of exultation came upon his face.

"It is," he said.

"Then pronounce the fatal words!"

Kamen Baka fell upon his knees and Rung his hands high above his head. The look in his face changed to one of agony.

"From henceforward, though all men love me, I love no man!"

The dark figure swept towards him and touched his head with her hand. "You are mine," she said, and turned away, a smile that was dark and cold like a northern frost upon her face. She gave me the idea of a teacher and a guide with Kamen; to Agmahd she had rather spoken as a queen might to her chief favourite, one whom she values and fears at once; one who has strength.

"Now, child, there is work to do," she said, approaching me. "This book has written in it the hearts of the priests who shall be my servants. Thou art weary and must rest, for I will not that they injure thee. Thou must grow to a strong man worthy of my favour. But carry the book with thee in thy arms; and as soon as thou shalt wake in the early morn Kamen shall come to thee, and thou shalt read to him the first page of this volume. When he has succeeded in accomplishing the first task, then he shall again come to thee at early morn and thou shalt read to him the second; and in this way the book will be finished. Tell him this; and bid him not despair at any time, because of difficulties. With each difficulty surmounted his power will increase, and when all is done he will stand supreme."

I repeated these words to Kamen. He was standing now at the doorway, his hands clasped in front of him, and his head drooped low, so that I could not see his face. But as I ceased, he raised his head and said, "I obey."

His face wore still the strange gleam which I had seen on it before.

"Bid him go," she said, "and he is to send Agmahd hither."

When I repeated this, he quietly withdrew; and I could see by his movements that the place to his eyes was all darkness.

A moment later and Agmahd stood in the doorway. She approached him and laid her hand upon his forehead. Immediately I saw a crown there; and Agmahd smiled.

"It shall be yours," she said. "Say this to Agmahd; it is the greatest crown but one upon the earth; and that greater one he would not wear. Now bid him carry thee in his arms and lay thee on thy couch. But thou clasp tight the book."

While I was repeating her words, she came to me and touched my forehead. A deep delicious languor came upon me, and I thought the words faded on my lips. But I could not say them again; all had vanished. I was asleep.

Chapter XI

When I awoke it was broad daylight; and I felt that I had slept a long deep sleep. My room was like a garden it was so full of flowers. My eyes wandered around them in pleasure, but presently lighted on an object which kept them fixed. It was a kneeling figure in the midst of the room; a priest whose head was bowed low; but I knew it was Kamen Baka. I moved, and at the slight sound I made he raised his head and looked towards me. In moving, I found that the book lay beside me open. My eyes became fastened to the page. I saw words that shone, and unconsciously I read them aloud. I ceased at last, because no more was writ in plain language, but all was hieroglyphics.

Kamen Baka started to his feet. I looked at him, and saw his face was all alight with what seemed like wild exultation.

"He shall kiss my feet to day," he cried out. Then observing my wondering gaze, he said, "Have you read all?"

"All that I can understand," I answered. "The rest is in strange characters that I do not know."

He turned instantly and left my chamber. I looked back at the page of the book which I had read to see what were the words which had so strangely excited him. They were now no longer intelligible to me—they too were writ in hieroglyphics—and I gazed at them in despair, for now I found I could remember no word of what I had read. I grew weary with puzzling over this strange thing, and at last I fell asleep again my head upon the open pages of the mystic book. I did not rouse from the deep dreamless sleep in which I was, until a sound startled me. Two young priests were in my room; they carried cakes and milk, and fell upon their knees to offer me the food. I was afraid, or I should have laughed to see them thus kneeling to me, a boy of the country. When I had eaten they left me, but I was not long alone. The curtain lifted, and at the sight of one who entered, I sprang to my feet and laughed with pleasure. It was Seboua, the gardener.

"How is it you have come to me?" I asked. "I thought indeed I was never to see you again."

"Agmahd sent me here," he said.

"Agmahd!" I cried in amazement. I approached him and pressed his arm between my hands.

"Oh yes, I am real," he answered. "They cannot make a phantom of me. Do not doubt when you see me it is I myself."

He spoke angrily and roughly, and for a moment I was afraid, but not for long. The strange smile came on his ugly face.

"You are to come with me into the garden" he said, and held out his dark large hand. I put mine in it, and together we left my room and went quickly away through the large empty chambers and long passages of the temple till we reached that narrow iron gateway through which I had first seen Seboua's face. As then so now, the garden shone beyond, a vision of greenness and light and colour.

"Oh! I am glad to come back here," I said.

"You came first to work; you were to be the drudge for me," said Seboua, proudly. "Now all's changed. You are to play, not work, and I am to treat you like a little prince.

Well! have they spoiled thee yet, I wonder, child? Wouldst like to bathe?"

"But where," I said, "in what waters? I would love to plunge in and swim in some water that was cool and deep."

"Thou canst swim? and thou lovest the water? Well, come with me and I will show thee deep water that will be cool indeed. Come thou with me!"

He walked on and I had to hurry to keep pace with him. He muttered to himself as he went, but I could not understand his words. Indeed, I did not listen for I was thinking of how glorious the plunge into cool water would be on this warm languid morning.

We came to a place where there was a wide, deep pool, into which water came dropping, dropping, in a quick swift shower from some place above.

"There is water for thee," said Seboua, "and no flowers are there for thee to hurt."

I stood on the brink in the warm sunlight and flung my white robe from me. Then with one instant of pause to look around and think how sweet the sun was, I plunged into the water. Ah! indeed, it was cold! My breath was almost gone with the sudden chill, but I struck out and began to swim, and soon began to glory in the sense of keen refreshment. I felt strong and eager, here in the sweet fresh waters. No longer languid as amid the fragrant odors of the temple, or the rich scents of the flowers in my chamber. I was so happy, I wanted to stay a long while here in the water mid the sun; so presently I ceased swimming and let myself float idly, and, closed my eyes that the sunlight should not blind me.

Suddenly I felt something so strange, I grew breathless, yet it was so gentle it did not terrify me. It was a kiss upon my mouth. I opened my eyes. There, beside me, lying upon the surface of the water, was my own Queen, the Lily

Queen, the Lady of the Lotus. I uttered a cry of joy. Immediately all pleasure which I had had since last I saw her vanished from my mind. She was my Queen, my beautiful friend; when she was there I had none other in all the world.

"Child, thou art come to me again" she said, "but soon thou wilt leave me; and how can I aid thee if thou forgettest me utterly?"

I made no answer, for I was ashamed. I could hardly believe that I had indeed forgotten and yet I knew that it was true.

"The waters thou liest in now," she said, "come from that place where my flowers, the lotus blossoms, dwell in their glory. Thou wouldst die wert thou to lie thus in the water where they dwell. But this that drops from them has but little of their life in it, and has given up its own to them. When thou must plunge into the water of the lotus tank, then thou wilt be strong as the eagle and eager as the young life of the newborn. My child, be thou strong; listen not to the flattery which confuses thee; listen only to the truth I keep in the sunlight, dear child, and let not the phantoms delude thee; for there is the life of lives awaiting thee, the pure flower of knowledge and love is ready for thee to pluck. Wouldst thou be a tool, a mere instrument in the hands of those who desire only for themselves? No! acquire knowledge and grow strong; then shalt thou be a giver of sunshine to the world. Come, my child, give me thine hand; rise in confidence, for this water will support thee; rise and kneel upon it and drink of the sunshine; rise and kneel upon it, and address thyself to the light of all life, that it may illumine thee."

I rose, holding her hand. I knelt beside her. I rose again and with her stood upon the water—and then I knew no more.

"Wouldst thou be a tool, a mere instrument in the hands of those who desire only for themselves? No! acquire knowledge and grow strong; then shalt thou be a giver of sunshine to the world."

These words seemed whispered in my ear as I awoke; I repeated them over and over, and remembered every separate word rightly. But they were vague and unmeaning to me; I had fancied I understood them when first I heard them, but now they sounded to me as the good words of the preacher sound to the dancers at the festivals.

*   *   *   *   *   *   *

I was a child when these words were breathed into my ear—a lad, helpless because ignorant and full of youth. Through the years of my growth, the cry to my soul from the Lily Queen rang dimly and without meaning in the obscure regions of my brain. They were to me as the song of the priest to the babe that hears but its music. Yet I never forgot them. My life was given up to the men who held me in bondage, in spirit and in body; fetters lay heavy on my unawakened soul. While my body yielded dully to the guidance of its masters, I was a slave, yet knew that freedom existed beneath the free sky! But, though I obeyed blindly, and gave all my strength and powers to the base uses of the desecrated temple, in my heart I held fast the memory of the beautiful queen and in my mind her words were written in fire that would not die. Yet as I grew to man's stature, my soul sickened within me. These words which lived like a star in my soul cast a strange light upon my wretched life. And as my mind developed I recognized this, and a heavy weariness, as of death or despair, shut away from me all the beauty of the world. From a gay child, a happy creature of sunshine, I grew into a sad youth, whose eyes were large and heavy with tears, and whose sick heart held hidden within it many secrets, but half understood, of shame and sin and sorrow. Sometimes, when I wandered through the garden I gazed into the still water of the lily tank and prayed to see again the vision. But it came not I had lost the innocence of childhood, and had not yet won the strength of the man.

Book II

Chapter I

I was in the garden of the temple, lying beneath a wide tree that cast deep shade upon the grass. I had been very weary, for all the night before I had been in the sanctuary, speaking the messages of the dark spirit to her priests. I slept a little in the warm air and awoke strangely full of sadness. I felt that my youth had gone, yet I had never enjoyed its fire.

On each side of me was a young priest. One was fanning me with a broad leaf that he must have plucked from the tree above. The other, leaning on one hand upon the grass, regarded me earnestly. His eyes were large and dark and pleasant, like the eyes of a kindly animal. I had often admired his beauty, and I was glad to see him at my side.

"You have been too much within doors. See now," he said, when he saw my eyes open wearily, and gaze into his face. "They shall not kill thee with the ceremonies of the temple, even if thou art the only one that can give them life. Wilt come into the town with us, and taste something different from the air of the temple?"

"But we cannot," I said.

"Cannot," said Malen contemptuously. "Do you suppose we are prisoners here?"

"But even if we can find a way out the people will know us. The priests do not go among the people."

"The people will not know us," said Malen with a merry laugh. "Agmahd has given us liberty. Agmahd has given us power. Come, if thou wilt—we are going."

The two rose and held out their hands to help me to rise; but I was no longer weak. I sprang to my feet, and arranged my white garment. "Are we to wear these robes?" I asked.

"Yes, yes, but none will know us. We shall appear as beggars, or as princes; what we will; Agmahd has given us power. Come!"

I was as delighted as they at this prospect of adventure. We ran across the garden till we came to a narrow gate in the wall. Malen touched it, and easily pushed it open. We were outside the temple.

My companions, laughing and talking as we went, ran across the plain to the city. I ran too, and listened; but I understood little of what they said. Evidently they knew the city, which to me was only a name. True, I had walked through it with my mother, a barefoot country lad. But now, it seemed, I was to enter houses, and mix with great and rich people. I felt afraid at the thought.

We hurried on until we entered one of the busiest streets. It was crowded with gay people in beautiful dresses, and all the shops seemed to sell only jewelry. Then we turned through a great gateway, into a courtyard, and from that passed into a marble hall where a great fountain played, and large flowering shrubs threw out a strong scent.

A wide marble stairway went out of this hall, and we immediately commenced to climb it. And when we reached the top Malen opened a door, and we entered a room all hung with golden tapestry, and where were a number of people whose dresses and jewels dazzled me. They were seated round a table drinking wine and eating sweetmeats. The air was full of talk and laughter, and heavy with perfume. Three very lovely women rose and welcomed us, each taking one of us by the hand, and giving us a place beside her. In a moment we seemed to be of the party, and to mingle our laughter with theirs, as though we had sat out all the feast. I know not whether it was the scented wine I drank or the magic touch of the beautiful hand that often touched mine, as it lay upon the embroidered table-cover—but my head grew light and strange, and I talked of things I did not know anything about till now, and laughed at sayings that an hour before would have seemed dull to me, because of my want of understanding.

She who sat next me pressed her hand in mine. I turned to look at her; she was leaning towards me; her face was brilliant with youth and beauty. Her rich dress had made me feel a child beside her, but now I saw that she was young, younger than myself, yet she was of such rich form and radiant loveliness that though a child in years she was a woman in charm. As I gazed into her tender eyes, it seemed to me that I knew her well, that her charm was familiar, and the stronger for its familiarity. She spoke many words that at first I hardly understood, indeed scarcely heard. But gradually, as I listened, I grew to understand. She told me of her longing for me in my absence, of her love for me, and of her weariness of all others on the earth. "The room seemed dark and silent till you came," she said. "The banquet had no mirth in it. The others laughed, but their laughter sounded as sobs in my ears—the sobs of those in torment. Is it for me, who am so young and strong and full of love, to be so sad? No—no, it is not for me. Ah, lover, husband, leave me not again alone. Stay by my side, and my passion will make thee strong to fulfill thy destiny."

I rose from my seat suddenly, holding her hand clasped tight in mine.

"It is true," I cried in a loud voice. "I have done ill to neglect that which is the glory of life. I confess it, that thy beauty, which indeed is mine, had been blotted from my mind. But now I see thee with mine eyes I wonder I could ever have seen beauty in aught else in heaven or earth."

Suddenly, while I spoke, there was a movement among the startled guests. With wonderful rapidity, they left the table and were at once gone from the room. Only the two young priests remained. Their eyes were fixed on me. They seemed grave, serious, disturbed. They rose slowly. "You will not return to the temple?" said Malen. My answer was a gesture of impatience. "Do you forget," he demanded, "that we were but to look at the follies of the city, that we might know of what clay men are made? You know that the initiated priests must retain their purity. What of you, the seer of the temple? Even I, who am but a novice, dare not yield the fierce longing for liberty that fills my soul. Ah, to be free! to be a child of the city, to know the meaning of life! But I dare not. Else am I less than nothing, I should have no place in the temple, no place in the world. How then will it be with thee, the seer? How are we to answer to Agmahd for thee?"

I made no answer. But she who sat beside me rose and advanced towards him. She took a jewel from her neck, and put it in his hand.

"Give him this," she said, "and he will ask no more."

Chapter II

From this hour there is a time of which I cannot give so careful an account as of the other days of my life. It is blurred and veiled by the similarity of the emotions through which I passed. Indeed, they merged together and became one and the same. I drank deep of pleasure each day; each hour it seemed to me that my beautiful companion grew more beautiful, so that I gazed upon her face in wonder. She led me through the rooms of our palace, and I could not stay to see their splendor, because always beyond were chambers yet more splendid. With her I wandered through the gardens, where the fragrant flowers grew in a profusion each as I had never seen in any other place. Beyond the gardens were meadows; in the short, sweet grass grew many wild flowers, and lilies blossomed in the stream that ran through the fields. Here the city maidens came at evening, some to fetch water, some to bathe in the stream and sit afterwards upon its bank, and talk and laugh and sing until the night was half spent. Their gleaming forms and sweet voices made the evenings doubly beautiful, and I would linger among them under the stars, and would often have stayed until the dawn the playmate of them all, but only whispering words of love to those who were most beautiful. And then, as they, singing in low voices, left me, she my own most beautiful went with me back to the palace, wherein we lived amid the city, yet apart from it. For we were happy as were none else within that city.

I cannot tell how long passed thus. Only I know that one day I lay within my own chamber, and she the most beautiful sang sweet low songs while her head lay upon my arm, when in a moment the song was hushed upon her lips and she lay pale and still. I heard, in the silence, a slow, soft footfall on the stairs. The door was opened, and Agmahd the high priest stood motionless within it.

He gazed at me one moment with his terrible eyes, that were cold as though they were jewels; there was a smile upon his face, but that smile struck me with fear, and I trembled.

"Come," he said.

I arose unhesitatingly. I knew that I must obey. I looked not back until I heard a swift movement and a sob; then I turned. But she, the most beautiful, was gone. Had she fled from before this unexpected appearance in our chamber? I could not stay to see, or go to comfort her. I knew that I must follow Agmahd; I felt as I had never felt before, that he was my master. As I came to the doorway, I saw across the threshold a snake that reared its head at my approach. I sprang back with a cry of horror.

Agmahd smiled. "Do not fear," he said. "This is a favourite of thy queen and will do her chosen servant no harm. Come!"

At his command I felt compelled to follow; I dared not disobey. I passed the snake with averted eyes, and as I reached the stairway I heard its hiss of anger.

Agmahd went through the gardens to the meadows beyond. It was evening, and already the stars were gleaming in the sky and the eyes of the maidens shone as they sat in groups by the side of the stream. But they did not sing as was their habit. In the midst of the stream was a boat, and in it two oarsmen. I recognized the young priests who had come with me to the city. Their eyes were downcast, and they did not raise them even at my approach. I understood as I passed by the girls that they had recognized old acquaintances and merry companions in those two young priests, and were amazed and full of wonder to see them in this dress, and of such changed demeanor.

Agmahd entered the boat; I followed him; and then we rowed silently towards the temple.

I had never seen the entrance to the temple from the water. I had heard when I was in the city with my mother that this entrance used to be often used, but now it was reserved only for festivals, so that I was much amazed to enter by this way. I was more amazed to find all the sacred precinct full of boats decorated with flowers and occupied, by white-robed priests, who sat with their eyes downcast. But I soon saw that today was a festival.

This temple! It seemed a hundred years since I had dwelled within it. Agmahd himself looked strange and unfamiliar to me. Was I indeed grown much older? I could not tell, for I found no mirror in which to see my face, and I found no friend to ask. Only this I knew, that compared with the youth who ran from the garden of the temple, eager for adventure, I was now a man. And I knew my manhood had, come to me not in glory, but in shame. I was a slave. A deep gloom settled on my soul as we entered the temple. The boat was drawn up to some wide white marble steps, which were within the walls of the temple and beneath its roof. I had never known the great river was so near. When we had reached the top of the steps, Agmahd opened a door, and lo! we were immediately at the entrance of the holy of holies. Only a few faint torches, held by silent priests, lit the great corridor. It was but dusk outside, on the river; here it was like deep night. At a sign from Agmahd the torches were extinguished. But all light was not gone!

for round the door of the sanctuary gleamed that strange light which once had so terrified me. It did not terrify me now. I knew what I had to do; and, unhesitatingly and without fear, I did it. I advanced, opened the door, and entered.

Within stood the dark figure, whose robes gleamed and whose eyes were cold and terrible. She smiled and put out her hand and laid it upon mine. I shuddered at the touch, it was so cold.

"Tell Agmahd," she said, "that I am coming. That I will be beside you in the boat. That he is to stand in the midst with us, and my other servants to surround us. And that then if all is done as I order, I will work a wonder before all the priests and before the people. And this I will do because I am well pleased with my servants, and because I desire them to have power and wealth."

I said her words again, and when I had ceased Agmahd's voice came out of the darkness.

"The Queen is welcomed! The Queen shall be obeyed."

A moment later and the torches were again lit. I saw that they were ten in number, carried by ten priests, who all wore white robes deeply embroidered in gold, as was that of Agmahd. Among them was Kamen Baka. His face looked strange to me. It was as the face of an ecstatic.

Agmahd opened the door which admitted us to the river steps. A different boat was moored here now. It was large, with a wide desk surrounded by vases, in which burned something strongly fragrant. Within these vases a circle was drawn in crimson and mingled with that a figure which I could not understand. At the sides of the boat, below this raised deck, sat the rowers—white-robed priests. All were still and mute, waiting with downcast eyes. The boat was hung with thick garlands of flowers, massed together till they seemed like great ropes. A lamp was burning at each end.

We entered the boat. Agmahd went first and stood in the midst of the circle. I took my place at his side. Between us, clearly visible to my eyes, was the figure. She shed a light like that which illumined the sanctuary, only less brilliant. But I saw that none perceived her presence but myself.

The ten priests entered the boat also, and placed themselves within the crimson circle, thus completely enclosing us. Then the boat slowly swung from the steps. I saw that a number of boats were before and behind us, all hung with flowers and lamps, all filled with white-robed priests. Silently the procession shot out upon the bosom of the sacred river and advanced towards the city.

When we were at last outside the temple, I heard a deep murmur rise and fill the air. It was so long and deep, it made me tremble with wonder but it disturbed none else, and soon I saw its meaning. As my eyes grew accustomed to the starlight, I saw that all the fields on each side of the river were full of a surging, swaying, mass of forms. A vast multitude of people crowded at the water's edge, and filled the fields as far as I could see. This was a great festival, and I had not known it. I wondered a while; but soon I remembered that I had, indeed, heard it spoken of, but I had been so saturated with the immediate pleasures about me that I had not heeded. Perhaps, had I remained in the city till now, I should have mingled in the crowd; but now I was isolated from the crowd, and, as it seemed to me, from all that was human. I stood silent and immovable as Agmahd himself. Yet, my soul was torn with a despair I could not understand, and crushed by a horror of the unknown which was yet to come.

Chapter III

As the boats glided down the river, suddenly the deep silence was broken by a burst of song. It came from the priests who rowed. From every boat the hymn rushed forth in a volume of sound, and I could see by the great movement, visible even in the dimness, that the people fell upon their knees. But they were silent; they adored and listened while the priests' voices rang out upon the air.

When the song ceased, there was a silence that was not broken for some minutes. The people remained motionless, kneeling, silent. But on a sudden they flung themselves prostrate upon the ground, and I would hear the sigh, the long breath of awe that came from the multitude: for the priests had burst out anew, with a cry of melodious triumph, and the words they uttered in so loud and strong a voice were these—

"The goddess is with us! She is in our midst! Fall down O people, and worship!"

At this moment the figure which stood between me and the priest Agmahd turned and smiled into my face.

"Now my chosen servant," she said, "I must ask your service. I have paid you beforehand that you might not hesitate. But do not fear. You shall be paid again and that doubly. Give me your hands. Place your lips upon my forehead, and fear not, move not, utter no cry, whatsoever faintness, whatsoever tremor come upon thee. Thy life will become mine. I shall draw it from thee: but I shall return it. Is it not precious? Do not fear."

I obeyed her without hesitation yet with dread unimaginable. But I could not resist her will I knew myself her slave. Her cold hands clasped mine, and instantly it seemed that they were no longer soft, but had become rivets of steel, which held me fast and were inexorable. Impelled by my sense of helplessness, I dared the glitter of these terrible eyes, and drew close to her. I longed for death to release me, but I could hope for no other help. I placed my lips upon her forehead. The vapour from the lamps and vessels had filled my brain with a strange sleepiness, and I was dull and heavy. But now, as my lips touched her forehead, which searched them, I knew not whether with cold or heat, a frenzied sense of joy, of lightness, of almost insane delight filled me. I knew myself no longer; I was swayed and dominated by a surging sea of emotions which were not my own. They swept through me, and their rush appeared to wash away my individuality utterly, and, as it then seemed, for ever. Yet I was not unconscious; my consciousness grew momently more intense and awake. Then in one strange second, I forgot the lost individuality—I knew that I was living in the brain, in the heart, in the essence of that being who had so utterly dominated me. A wild cry, instantly hushed, rang out from the people. They saw their goddess. And I, looking down saw at my feet the seemingly dead form of a young priest, robed in white garments, gold-embroidered. I paused for one instant, in my joy of power to wonder, Was he dead?

Chapter IV

I could see the great multitude which was on each side clearly; a light fell upon them which they did not perceive. It was not the starlight by which they saw, but a brilliance that came not from the heavens but from my eyes. I saw their hearts—I saw not their bodies but themselves. I recognized my servants, and my soul lifted itself as I perceived that nearly all of this multitude were ready to serve me. Mine was a worthy army; they would obey, not from duty but desire.

I saw in each heart what was its hunger, and I knew that I could feed it. One long moment I remained visible; then I left my chosen servants. I bade them draw near to the shore; for now that I was no longer intent upon making myself seen by these dull eyes of men, I could speak to and touch those whom I chose. The strong life of the young priest was enough to feed the lamp of physical power for some time if I did not use it too swiftly.

I stepped upon the shore, and moved among the people, speaking into the ear of each the secret of his heart—more, I told him how to obtain that which he only thought of silently. No man or woman was without some longing which shame would have held them forever from uttering even to a confessor. But I saw it, and made it no longer a thing of shame, and showed how small an effort of will, how slight a knowledge was needed for the first step in self-gratification. All through the throng I went, hither and thither, and as I passed I left a maddened and impassioned crowd behind me. At length the intoxication which my presence produced could no longer be held in check. With one voice the people burst out into a wild song that thrilled my blood, and made it burn within me. Have I not heard this song under other skies, sung in the voices and languages of all peoples? Have I not heard it from peoples who are long since extinct and forgotten? Shall I not hear it from peoples whose dwelling-places are not yet created? It is my song! It gives me life! Uttered silently in one heart, it is the cry of the unspoken passion the hidden madness of self. When it comes from the throat of the multitude, shame is gone and concealment at an end. Then it is the frenzied utterance of the organ, the outcry of the devotees of pleasure.

My work was done. I had lit a great fire which raged on like the fire in the forest. I turned back to the sacred boat where it awaited me. Motionless they stood there, waiting my return those my chosen servants, the high priests of the temple. Ah, my mighty ones in passion! Kings in lust! Monarchs in desire!

And the young priest—was he still there? Still looking like one dead? Yes, he lay motionless, pallid, in the midst of the circle formed by the high priests, lying at the feet of Agmahd, who stood here alone.

As this thought came to me, I seemed suddenly to withdraw myself in some mysterious way from the sea of passion in which I had been submerged. I knew myself again—that I was not the goddess, but had been only absorbed by her, sucked up into her embracing personality. Now I was again separated from her. But I did not return to that pale shape which so lifelessly lay upon the deck of the sacred boat. I was in the temple; I was in darkness; yet I knew that I was in the holy of holies.

A light came in the darkness. I looked, and, lo! the inner cave was full of light: and within it stood the Lady of the Lotus.

I was at the door of the inner cave, close to her, within the glance of her eyes. I tried to escape—I tried to turn—I could not. I trembled as I had never trembled before even with horror or dread.

For she stood silently, her eyes upon me. And I saw that they were full of a great anger. And she who had been to me a tender friend, gentle as a kind mother, now stood in her majesty before me, and I knew that I had angered a god the most to be dreaded of all that are known to men.

"Was it for this, O Sensa! beloved of the gods! that thou wert born? Was it for this that thine eyes were opened and thy senses made clear to perceive? Thou knowest it was not; yet those seeing eyes and those swift senses have at last served their master, and shown thee who and what it is thou hast been serving. Wilt thou serve her always? Now that thou art a man, choose! Art thou fallen so low that thou wilt be a slave forever? Go, then! I have come to cleanse my sanctuary. I will endure no longer. It shall be silent, and the people shall not know that any god exist, rather than that they shall be lied to by false lips, and tempted by the darkness. Go! None shall enter here again. I close the door! The sanctuary is dumb, and knows no voice. I sit here alone and silent; yea, through the ages I will dwell here without speech, and the people shall say I am dead. Be it so! In the ages to come my children will rise again and the darkness shall break. Oh! Thou hast chosen! Fall! Thy estate is lost. Leave me to my silence!"

She raised her hand with a gesture that bade me leave her. It was so imperative, so royal, that I could not disobey. I turned, I drooped my head, I went with sad steps to the outer door of the sanctuary. Yet I could not open it; I could not pass out; I could advance no further. My heart turned sick within me and held me back. I fell on my knees and cried out in a voice of agony, "Mother! Queen and Mother!"

A moment passed in an awful silence, I waited, I knew not for what. My soul was hungry and desperate. An awful memory came to me in the darkness and silence. I saw in the past not only pleasure, but deeds. I saw that I had done these blindly, accepting the stupefaction of my soul as men accept the dulness of wine. And I had done the work given me to do in a stupor, thinking not of it, but of the rewards, of each pleasure that was to come. I had been the mouthpiece, the oracle of her, that black soul, whom now I had seen and whom now I knew. The past grew so terrible, so present, so fierce in its denunciation that again I cried out in the darkness, "Mother! Save me!"

A touch came on my hand and on my face. I heard a voice in my ear and in my heart, "Thou art saved. Be strong." And the light came upon my eyes, but I could not see, for a rain of tears washed from them the frightful visions they had seen.

Chapter V

I was no longer in the sanctuary. I felt the air on my face. I opened my eyes and saw the sky above me, and the shining stars in its depth. I was lying prostrate, and I felt strangely weary. Yet I was roused by the sound of a thousand voices, whose cries and songs struck on my ears. What could this be?

I raised myself. I was in the midst of the circle of priests, of the ten high-priests. Agmahd stood beside me; he was watching me. My eyes fixed on his face, and I could not look away. Pitiless, heartless, soulless! Had I feared him? This image, this unhuman being? I feared him no longer. I looked round at the priests who surrounded me. I read their faces; they were absorbed, self-conscious. Each and all were bitten and eaten by one deep desire, one hunger for gratification which he cherished like a serpent, next his heart. I could no longer fear these men. I had seen the light. I was strong.

I rose to my feet. I looked round at the multitudes who crowded the banks of the river, beneath the clear sky. I understood then the strange voices I had heard. The people were mad; some with wine, some with love, some with absolute frenzy. Numbers of small boats had crowded the water; the people had come in these to make offerings to the goddess whom they adored, and whom to-night they had seen and heard, and felt. The sacred boat on which I stood was weighted and heaped with the offerings the people had flung into it, standing up in their low vessels, their rafts, by the side of ours. Gold and silver, jewels, and vessels of gold set with shining stones. Agmahd looked at these things, and I saw the smile on his lips. These riches might feed the temple, but for himself it was very different jewels he desired and worked for. My soul spoke suddenly unawares. I could look on and be silent no longer. I spoke in a loud voice, and commanded the people to hear me, and immediately there was a stillness which grew till it spread over the multitude.

"Listen to me, you that are worshippers here, of the goddess. What goddess is it you worship? Can you not tell by the words she whispers into your hearts? Look within and if she has seared you with the fierce heat of passion know she is no true god! For there is no truth save in wisdom. Listen and I will speak to you words that have been uttered in the sanctuary, and breathed by the spirit of light, our Queen Mother. Know that in virtue, in true thoughts, in true deeds, only can you find peace. Is this dark organ a fit surrounding for the goddess of truth? Are you her worshippers, who are drunk with wine and passion here beneath the open sky? You with wild words of impiety and frenzied songs on your lips, and thoughts of shame at your hearts, ready to spring boldly into deeds? No! down on your knees, and lift your hands to heaven and ask that beneficent spirit, our queen of wisdom, who broods over you with wide wings of love, to forgive your shamelessness, to help you in a new effort. Hear me. I will pray to her, for I see her in her splendor. Speak to her the words I utter, and she shall surely listen for she loves you even though you offend—"

A burst of melody, a number of strong voices singing, drowned my voice. The priests had burst out into song with the rich music of a hymn. The people, swayed by my voice and words, had in masses fallen upon their knees. Now, intoxicated by the music, they sang the hymn with fervor, and the volume of sound rose majestically into the sky. A strong sweet scent entered my nostrils. I turned from it with dislike, but already it had done its work. I felt my brain swoon.

"He is in an ecstasy," said Kamen Baka.

"He is mad," I heard uttered in another voice—a voice so cold, so enraged, I hardly recognized it. Yet I knew it was Agmahd who spoke.

I strove to answer him, for I was inspired in all I did by a new and strange courage, and I knew nothing of fear. But already the stupefying vapour had done its work. I was dumb, as in sleep; my head grew heavy. In a few seconds I was asleep.

Chapter VI

When I awoke I was in my old chamber in the temple; the one in which my first boyish terrors came to me. I was very tired; so tired that the first sensation I experienced was that of intolerable weariness, which numbed all my body. I lay still a little while, thinking only of my discomfort.

Then suddenly the events of yesterday came into my memory. It was like the rising of the sun. I had found her again, my Queen Mother, and she had taken me back to her protection.

I rose, forgetting my pain and weariness. It was just dawn and through the high window the faint gray light came softly into my room. It was brilliant with rich material and rich embroidery; full of strange and beautiful things which made it seem like a chamber for a prince. But for its peculiar shape and the high window, it could hardly have been recognized as the room which in my childhood had been made a garden of flowers for my pleasure.

The air within seemed to me heavy and dull; I longed to be outside, in the air, sweet with the newness of morning; for I felt that I too needed to be new-made and strong with the strength of youth. And here the perfumed atmosphere, the heavy draperies and weight of luxury, oppressed me.

I lifted the curtain and crossed the great room which was next mine. It was empty and silent; so was the wide corridor. I went softly on through the long corridors, till I reached that in which the gate opened to the garden. Through the iron grating I could see the gleam of the grass as I approached it. Ah, that beautiful garden! Oh, to bathe in that sweet water of the lily tank!

But the iron door was fast locked; I could but look through all the grass and sky and flowers, and drink the sweet air in through the narrow openings. Suddenly I saw Seboua approaching down one of the garden walks. He came straight to the iron door within which I stood.

"Seboua!" I cried.

"Ah, thou art here," he said, speaking in his rough tones. "The man and the child are alike. But no longer may Seboua be thy friend. I have failed, and I may not try again. I angered both my masters when you were a child; I could not hold you fast for either. Be it so; you must now stand alone."

"Can you not open the gate?" was all my answer.

"No," he said; "and I doubt if it will ever be opened for thee again. What matters it? Art thou not the favourite priest of the temple, the darling, the cherished one?"

"No," I answered, "I am that no longer. They already say I am mad. They will say it again to-day."

Seboua looked at me earnestly. "They will kill you!" he said in a low voice full of tenderness and pity.

"They cannot," I answered, smiling. "My Queen will protect me. I must live till I have spoken all she wishes. Then I care not."

Seboua raised his hand from where it had remained hidden in the folds of his black dress. He held in it a bud of the lotus flower that lay in a green leaf which seemed its bed.

"Take it," he said. "It is for thee; it speaks a language that thou wilt understand. Take it, and may good go with thee. I that am dumb, save in common speech, yet am worthy to be a messenger. That makes me glad. But thou mayst rejoice, for thou canst hear and speak, learn and teach."

Immediately he was gone; while he had been speaking he had pushed the flower to me through one of the narrow openings of the grating. I drew it towards me carefully. I held it now in my hands; I was content. I needed nothing else.

I went back to my room and sat down holding the flower in my hand. It was the same thing over again as when I had, long ago, a mere child, sat in this same chamber, holding a lily and gazing into its centre. I had a friend, a guide; a union with that unseen Mother of Grace. But now I knew the value of what I held; then I did not. Was it possible that it would be again taken from me so easily? Surely no.

For I could understand its language now. Then it spoke to me of nothing save its own beauty; now it opened my eyes, and I saw; it unsealed my ears, and I heard.

A circle was round me; such as had surrounded me when I had taught, unknowingly, in the temple. These were priests, white-robed, as those had been who knelt and worshipped me. But these did not kneel; they stood and gazed down upon me with profound eyes of pity and love. Some were old men stately and strong; some were young and slender, with faces of fresh light. I looked round in awe, and trembled with hope and joy.

I knew, without any words to tell me, what brotherhood this was. These were my predecessors, the priests of the sanctuary, the seers, the chosen servants of the Lily Queen. I saw that they had succeeded each to each, keeping sacredly the guardianship of the holy of holies since first it was shaped out of the great rock, against which the temple rested.

"Art ready to learn?" said one to me—one whose breath seemed to me to be drawn from long-forgotten ages.

"I am ready," I said; and knelt upon the ground in the centre of that strange, holy circle. My body fell, yet my spirit seemed to soar. Though I knelt, I knew I was held up in soul by those who surrounded me. Henceforth they were my brethren.

"Sit thou there," he said, pointing to my couch, "and I will talk with thee."

I rose, and turning to go to the couch, saw that I was alone with this one who spoke to me. The others had left us. He came and sat beside me, and began to speak. He poured into my heart the wisdom of the dead ages; wisdom which lives forever, and is young when the race of its early disciples is no longer even a memory. My heart grew green with the freshness of this ancient knowledge and truth.

Throughout that day he sat beside me and taught. At night he touched my forehead with his hands and left me. As I lay down to sleep, I recollected that I had seen none but my teacher since yesterday, nor had I tasted food. Yet I was not weary with learning, nor was I faint. I laid my flower beside me, and slept quietly.

When I awoke I started up, fancying some one touched my flower. But I was alone, and my flower was safe. A table stood near the heavy curtain which separated my room from the next; on this table stood food; milk and cakes. All yesterday I had not eaten: I was glad now of the food. I put my flower within my dress, and went to the table. I drank the milk and ate the cakes; and then with new strength in me, I turned to go to my couch, and there meditate earnestly on what I had learned yesterday, for I knew that these were golden seeds which must bear fruits of glory.

But I stood still and my heart sank within me; for again I was surrounded by the beautiful circle. He who had taught me yesterday, looked at me and smiled, but he did not speak. Another approached me, took my hand and led me to the couch, and I was alone with him.

Alone, yet not alone, and never to be any longer alone, for he took my heart and soul, and showed them to me in their nakedness, unsoftened by any fancied sanctity. He took my past, and showed it to me in its simple, dark, unbeautiful poverty; that past which might have been so rich. Until now, it seemed to me I had been living in unconsciousness. Now, I was guided through my own life again and bidden regard it with clear vision. The chambers I passed through were dark and dreary; some of them were full of horrors. For now I saw that I had been won by the magic which I myself had interpreted to Kamen Baka. Like the others, I had existed for desire and its satisfaction. And steeped in the joys of pleasure, of beauty, I had been as one intoxicated, and I knew not all that I did. Remembering my past, I saw the meaning of Seboua's words, which at the time I hardly understood. I had indeed been the darling of the temple, for when my body was steeped in pleasure, and silenced in the dim sleep of satiety, my lips and voice had become docile to the will of that dark mistress. Through my physical powers she made known her wishes, and obtained the service of those slaves who had bartered their all for the sake of gratification. By her fierce and terrible insight into the dark caverns of men's souls, she saw their needs, and with my speech she showed them how to obtain that which they longed for.

As I sat there, dumb and amazed at the visions which passed through my awakened memory, I saw myself first, a mere child, lulled from terror and alarm by pleasure. I saw myself within the temple, in its inner sanctuary, a creature helpless, a tool, a mere instrument played upon mercilessly. I saw myself later, a youth fresh and beautiful, lying unconscious on the deck of the sacred boat, rising in the frenzy of unconsciousness, and uttering strange words. I saw myself later, grown pale and faint, yet always the willing instrument, although the soul was beginning to stir and weary the body with its struggle; and now I saw that the soul had awakened, had touched its mother, the queen of light, and could never again be silenced.

The night came, and my teacher left me. None else had come to my chamber; no food had been brought to me since the early morning. I was faint with the terrible sights which I had seen in this short day. I determined to go in search of the food I needed. I lifted the heavy curtain that covered the archway, which led into the great room beyond. A door was there—a massive door—such as might close the portal of a dungeon. Then I understood I was a prisoner, and now that I had recovered from my weakness and excitement, I was to have no food. Agmahd had seen that my spirit had awakened; he had determined to kill it within me, and preserve the mere broken body for his purpose.

I lay down upon my couch, and fell asleep with the drooping lily-bud upon my lips.

When I awoke, one stood beside me whom I knew to be my new teacher. I had met his smile when I had seen the beautiful circle around me. I sprang up gladly; from him I looked, for encouragement. He came and sat beside me, and took my hand in his.

And then I knew that his smile was the light of a great peace. He had died in this chamber—died for the truth. He called me brother, and suddenly I became aware that the roses of my life had blown and fallen and passed away forever. I had to live for the truth in the light of the pure spirit, and no suffering must make me afraid, and from the moment that his hand touched mine, I knew that no suffering could make me afraid. Until now, pain had always blinded me with terror, but now I knew that I could meet and grasp it with strong hands unterrified. I sank to sleep that night in an ecstasy; I knew not whether I waked or dreamed; but I knew that this my brother, whose physical life had been torn from him in the long ages past, had poured the strength of his fiery soul into mine, and that I could never lose it again.

Chapter VII

On the morrow when my eyes opened my bed was surrounded by the beautiful circle. They regarded me with grave looks; I saw no smile on any face; but the infinite tenderness which I felt from them gave me strength. I rose and knelt beside my couch, for I saw that some great moment was approaching.

The youngest and the brightest of them all left the circle and approached me. He knelt beside me and clasped my hands, holding within them the faded lotus blossom which lay upon my pillow.

I looked up—the others were gone. I regarded my companion. He was silent; his eyes were fixed on me. How young he was and beautiful! Earth had left no soil on his spirit. I knew that its stain must be on mine until in the course of ages I had washed it clean again. I felt a fear of this my companion, he was so white and spotless.

As we remained thus in silence a soft voice fell on my ear.

"Look not up yet," whispered he who knelt at my side.

"Twin stars of the evening, thou the last of the long line of seers who have made the wisdom of the Temple and crowned the greatness of Egypt with glory! The night is at hand, and the darkness must fall and hide the earth from the beauty of the heavens above it. Yet the truth shall be left with my people, the ignorant children of earth. And it is for you to leave behind you a burning light, a record for all time which men shall look at and wonder at in ages hence. The record of your lives, and of the truth which inspired you, shall go to other races, in other parts of the dim earth, to a people who have only heard of the light, who have never seen it. Be strong, for your work is great. Thou, my child of the snowy soul, thou hadst not strength to battle alone with the growing darkness; but now, give of thy faith and purity to this one, whose wings are smirched with stains of the earth, but who has gathered from that dark contact strength for the coming battle. Fight thou to the last for thy Queen Mother. Speak to my people, and tell them of the great truths; tell them that the soul lives and is blessed, unless they drown it in degradation; tell them there is freedom and peace for all who will free themselves from desires; tell them to look to me and find rest in my love; tell them there is the lotus-bloom in every human soul, and that it will open wide to the light unless they poison its roots; tell them to live in innocence and seek after truth, and I will come and walk in their midst, and show them the way into that place of peace where all is beauty and all are content. Tell them I love my children and would come and dwell in their homes and bring that content which is more than any prosperity, even unto these their hearths of the earth. Tell them this in a voice like a trumpet-call, which cannot be misunderstood. Save those who will hear, and make my temple once more a dwelling for the Spirit of Truth. The temple must fall, but it shall not fall in iniquity. Egypt must decay; but it shall not decay in ignorance. It shall hear a voice it cannot forget; and the words which that voice utters shall be the hidden heirloom of ages, and shall again be spoken under another sky, and herald the dawn which must break through the long blackness. Thou, my youngest, thou who art both strong and weak, prepare! The struggle is at hand; do not flinch. One duty is thine; to teach the people. Do not fear that wisdom shall fail thy tongue. I, who am Wisdom, will speak in thy voice. I, who am Wisdom, will be at thy side. Look up, my child, and gather strength."

I raised my eyes, and as I did so felt the tightened grasp of the hand of my companion who knelt at my side. I understood that he desired to give me courage to face the blinding glory which was before my eyes.

She stood before us, and I saw her as the flower sees the sun which feeds it. I saw her without disguise or veil. The fair woman who had soothed my boyish tears was lost in the god, the glory of whose presence filled my soul with a burning that seemed to me like death. Yet I lived; I saw; I understood.

Chapter VIII

The beautiful young priest rose and stood beside me, while I still gazed upon the glory.

"Hear me, my brother," he said. "There are three truths which are absolute, and which cannot be lost, but yet may remain silent for lack of speech.

"The soul of man is immortal, and its future is the future of a thing whose growth and splendor has no limit.

"The principle which gives life dwells in us, and without us, is undying and eternally beneficent, is not heard or seen or smelt, but is perceived by the man who desires perception.

"Each man is his own absolute lawgiver, the dispenser of glory or gloom to himself; the decreer of his life, his reward, his punishment.

"These truths, which are as great as is life itself, are as simple as the simplest mind of man. Feed the hungry with them. Farewell. It is sundown. They will come for you; be thou ready."

He was gone. But the glory did not fade from before my eyes. I saw the truth. I saw the light. I remained, holding the vision with my passionate regard.

Some one touched me. I was awakened and stirred immediately by a sudden startling sense that the hour of battle had come. I rose and looked round. Agmahd stood beside me. He looked very serious; his face was less cold than was usual; there was a fire in his eyes such as I had never seen there before.

"Sensa," he said in a low voice, very clear, that seemed like a knife, "art thou prepared? To-night is the last night of the Great Festival. I need your service. When last you were with us you were mad; your brain was frenzied with the follies of your own conceit. I demand your obedience now, as you have hitherto given it, and to-night you are needed, for a great miracle has to be worked. You must be passive, else you will suffer. The Ten have determined that, unless you are obedient as hitherto, you must die. You are too well versed in all we know to live, unless you are one of us. Your choice lies plain before you. Make it quickly."

"It is made," I answered.

He looked at me very earnestly. I read his thought, and saw that he had expected to find me sad with solitude, sick with the long fast, and broken in spirit. Instead, I stood erect, unexhausted, filled with fearlessness; I felt that the light was in my soul, that the great army of the glorious ones stool behind me.

"I have no fear of death," I answered; "and I will no longer be the tool of men who are killing the royal religion of Egypt, the great and only religion of truth, for the benefit of their own ambitions and desires. I have seen and understood your miracles and the teachings which you give to the people; I will aid you no longer I have said."

Agmahd stood silent, regarding me. His face grew whiter and more rigid, as though cut in marble. I remembered his words that night in the inner sanctuary, when he said, "I renounce my humanity." I saw it was so, that the renunciation was complete. I could look for no mercy; I had to deal not with man but with a shape animated by a dominant and absolutely selfish will.

After a moment's pause he spoke, very calmly—

"Be it so. The Ten shall hear your words and answer them; you have a right to be present at their deliberations; you are yourself as high in the temple as I myself. It will be a trial of strength against strength, of will against will. I warn you that you will suffer."

He turned away and left me, moving with that slow and stately step which had so fascinated me when a child.

I sat down upon my couch and waited. I was not afraid; but I could not think or reflect. I was conscious that a moment was at hand which would need all my strength; and I remained without motion and without thought, reserving all the force I possessed.

A star rose in front of me, a gleaming star, which seemed to me shaped like the full-blown lotus flower. Excited and dazzled, I rose and sprang towards it. It moved from me— I would not lose it, but followed eagerly. It passed through the doorway of my room into the corridor; I found that the door opened at my touch. I did not stay to wonder why it was unlocked, but followed the star and its light, which momently grew clearer, and its shape grew more defined; I saw the petals of the royal white flower, and from its yellow centre streamed the light that led me.

Swiftly and eagerly I went down the wide dim corridor. The great door of the temple was open and the star passed through it into the outer air. I too went out of the temple door, and found myself in the avenue of strange statues. Suddenly I became aware that there was a presence at the outer gate which called me. I fled down the long avenue with feet that knew not whither they led me; yet I knew that I must go. The great gates were locked; but, so close to them that I felt as though I were in the midst of it, was a great crowd, a mass of people. They were awaiting the great ceremony, the final glory of the festival, which to-night was to take place at the portals of the temple itself. I looked up and saw the Queen Mother standing beside me. She had, in her hand a flaming torch, and I knew that its light had formed the star which guided me hither. She it was, then, the light of life, who had led me. She smiled and was, in an instant, gone; I was alone with my knowledge; and the people, crowded together and plunged in ignorance, waited at the gates to be taught of the priests.

I remembered the words of my predecessor, my brother, who had given me the three truths for the people.

I lifted up my voice and spoke; my words carried me on as though they were waves, and my emotion grieve into a great sea upon which I was lifted; and as I looked into the eager eyes and rapt wondering faces before me, I knew that the people also were being swept along on that swift tide. My heart swelled with the delight of speech, of giving utterance to the great truths which had become my own.

At last I began to tell them how I had caught fire from the torch of holiness, and was resolved to enter upon a true life of devotion to wisdom, and to discard all the luxury which surrounded the priestly life, and to put aside forever all desires but those which belong to the soul. I cried aloud, praying all those who felt the light kindle within them, to enter upon a similar path, even in the midst of their life in the city or on the mountains. I told them that it was unnecessary because men bought and sold in the streets, that they should utterly forget and drown the divine essence within them. I bade them burn out by the light of the spirit the grosser desires of the flesh which held them back from the true doctrine, and sent them in throngs as devotees to the shrine of the Queen of Desire.

I paused suddenly with a heavy sense of weariness and exhaustion. I became aware that some one stood on each side of me; an instant later, I saw that I was surrounded.

The ten high priests had formed a circle around me. Kamen Baka stood facing me, and fixed his eyes on mine.

I cried out aloud, standing there in the midst of this circle—

"O, people of Egypt, remember my words! Never again may you hear the messenger of the mother of our life, the mother of the God of Truth. She has spoken. Go to your homes and write her words on tablets, and grave them on stones, that people yet unborn may read them and repeat them to your children that they shall know of the wisdom. Go, and stay not to witness the sacrilege of the temple which is to-night to be committed. The priests of the goddess desecrate her temple with madness and lust and rich filling of all desires. Listen not to their words, but go to your homes and ask of your own hearts their lesson."

My strength was gone. I could utter no word more. With drooped head and weary limbs, I obeyed the menacing circle which surrounded me, and turned my steps towards the temple.

In silence we moved up the avenue, and entered the doorway. Within it we paused. Kamen Baka turned and looked back down the avenue.

"The people murmur," he said.

Again we moved on down the great corridor. Agmahd came out of a doorway, and stood before us.

"Is it so?" he said in a strange voice. He knew what had happened by the group he regarded.

"What shall be done?" said Kamen Baka. "He betrays the secrets of the temple, and excites the people against us."

"He will be a great loss," said Agmahd, "but he has become too dangerous. He must die. Speak I well, brethren?"

A faint murmur passed round me from lip to lip. Every voice was with Agmahd.

"The people murmur at the gate," repeated Kamen Baka.

"Go to them," said Agmahd, "tell them this is a night of sacrifice, and the goddess will herself speak with her own voice."

Kamen Baka left the circle, and Agmahd immediately took his place. I stood motionless, silent. I dimly understood that my fate was sealed, but I neither knew nor desired to ask in what way I was to die. I knew myself to be utterly helpless in the hands of the high priests. There was no appeal from their authority, and the crowd of inferior priests obeyed them as slaves. I, one alone, was helpless amid this crowd, and under this absolute authority. I did not fear death, and I thought it due to the Queen Mother that her servant should go to her with all gladness. It was my last testimony on earth to her love.

Chapter IX

I was taken into my own chamber, and there left alone. I lay down upon my couch and fell asleep, for I was very weary, and I was not afraid, it seemed to me that under my head was the tender arm of the Lady of the Lotus.

But my sleep was short. I was plunged in a deep unconsciousness, that was too sweet for any dream to enter, when suddenly I was roused by a vivid sense of being no longer alone. I awoke to find myself in darkness and silence, but I recognized the sensation. I knew I was surrounded by a great crowd. I waited motionless with watchful eyes for the light, wondering what presences it would reveal to me.

Then I became aware of something I had never felt before. I was not unconscious, yet I was helpless as though without sense or knowledge. I was not motionless from indifference or peacefulness. I desired to rise and demand that light should be brought, but I could neither move nor utter any sound. Some fierce will was battling with mine, so strong that I was all but utterly mastered, yet I struggled and would not yield. I was determined not to be a blind slave, overpowered in the darkness by an unseen adversary.

It became terrible, this fight for supremacy. It became so fierce that at last I knew it was a fight for my life. The power that weighed me down desired to kill. What was it, who was it, that endeavoured to draw my breath from out my body?

At last—I cannot tell how long this intense silent warfare was waged—at last the light came flashing round me on every side, as torch was lighted from torch. I saw dimly, for my sight was faint. I saw that I was in the great corridor before the door of the sanctuary, lying upon the couch where I had played with the strange phantom-child who first taught me pleasure. I lay upon it outstretched as I had lain on my own couch in sleep. As when it had been used in the ceremonial before, so now it was covered with roses—large, rich, voluptuous, crimson and blood-red roses; thousands lay upon and about the couch, and their strong perfume overpowered my faint senses. I was clothed strangely in a thin white linen robe, whereon were embroideries, such as until now I had never seen hieroglyphs worked in thick, dark, red silk. At my side was a stream of red blood, which flowed from the couch into a beautiful vessel that stood upon the ground amid a heap of roses. I looked at this a while in idle curiosity, until on a sudden the knowledge came to me that this was my life's blood flowing away.

I raised my eyes, and saw that I was surrounded by the Ten. Their gaze was all fixed on me, their countenances were implacable. I knew then what that terrible will was with which I had done battle. It was their united resolution. Was it possible that I alone could struggle against this band? I knew not, yet I was not cast down. By one great effort I raised myself on the couch. I was already weak from want of blood, but they could no longer keep me silent. I rose to my feet, and stood upon the couch, and looked past them to the crowd of priests beyond, and further still to the throng of people, who waited close-packed at the entrance of the great corridor, to see the promised miracle.

I stood one instant, and thought I had power to speak, but I fell back helpless in my weakness. Yet a deep, profound, vivid happiness filled my soul, and suddenly I heard a murmur which rose and grew stronger.

"It is the young priest that taught at the gate! He is good, he shall not die! Let us save him!"

The people had seen my face and knew me. A great rush was made in the sudden enthusiasm, and the crowd of priests was pressed towards the couch, so that the Ten were unable to remain around it. And as the wave of struggle came up towards the holy of holies, many of the priests rushed into the vacant space between the couch and the door. And as they passed by in the confusion and surprise, I saw that the vessel which held my life was overturned and the red blood was spilled at the door of the sanctuary. The door opened; Agmahd stood within it; he looked majestic in his impenetrable calm. He gazed upon the surging crowd before him. At his cold gaze the priests grew calmer and gathered strength to withstand a little longer the onrush of the crowd. The Ten drew together again and with difficulty reached my couch and again formed a barrier about it.

But they were too late. Already some of the people had reached my side. I smiled dimly into their kindly rough faces. Tears fell upon my face and penetrated my heart; and then suddenly one caught my hand and clasped and kissed it, and wetted it with hot tears. Surely that touch thrilled my blood as did none other! Then I heard a voice cry: "It is my son—it is my son that is dead. He is killed. Who will give me back my son?

It was my mother who knelt at my side. I strained my fading sight and saw her. She was worn and weary, yet her face was good. And as I looked I saw behind her, overshadowing her, the Lady of the Lotus, standing there in the midst of the people! And a gentle smile was on her mouth.

My mother rose, and I saw a strange dignity in her face.

"They have killed his body," she said, "but they have not killed his soul. That is strong, for I saw it in his eyes as this moment they closed in death."

Chapter X

And on my dim ears fell the sound of a great sigh that came from the heart of the people. And then I knew that my body did not die in vain.

But my soul lived. It was not only strong, it was indestructible. It had worked out its time of misery in that pale form; it had escaped from the imprisonment which so long had held it fast. But only to reawaken in another, a strong, a beautiful and pure temple.

As the great surging crowd, driven to fury by the resistance of the priests, pressed on menacingly, some victims to its rage fell around me. Close to my lifeless form lay Agmahd, trampled to death by the enraged people, and at my very side against the couch on which I lay, Malen died, his breath pressed out from his beautiful form. As I hovered there in the strange consciousness of soul, I perceived these tainted spirits, dark with the lust and ambition which the Queen of Desire had kindled within them, forced into that circle of necessity from which there is no escape. Agmahd's soul fled with a fierce rush, like the dark passage of a bird of the night, and Malen that young priest, who had led me to the city, followed him swiftly. He, who obedient to the rules of his order had preserved the purity of the body, was black within with ungratified and ceaseless desire, but his body lay a broken flower, fair as a lily when first it opens its bloom on the surface of the clear water.

I felt that my Queen Mother held me fast in her tender grasp, that I might not escape from the scene of horror.

"Return to your work," she said; "it is yet unfinished. This is the new robe that you will wear, which will be your covering while you teach my people. This body is sinless, unstained and beautiful, although the soul that inhabited it is lost. But thou art my own. To come to me is to live through eternity in truth and knowledge. This is thy new garment."

I found that I was yet strong, not only in the spirit, but in physical life. New vigour came to me, my weariness was forgotten. I rose from the place, where but a minute since I had lain prostrate and lifeless. I rose, and standing hidden under the eyes of my Queen looked in horror at the scene around me.

"Go, Malen go in safety," she said. "Thou art to live in the hearts of the people, thou wilt be to them an image and symbol of the glory. Thou wilt be again a martyr to my cause, one who will forever be remembered with love by the dusky children of Chemi. Yet, though thou diest in my service, thou shalt teach for ages to come among the ruins of this temple; and though thou diest for me a hundred deaths, yet shalt thou live to teach my truths from the adytum of the new fane that shall arise in the distance of time."

I hurried away, and passed unnoticed through the surging, furious crowd. The statues in the avenue were thrown down; the temple gates were broken and destroyed.

My soul was sad and yearned for peace. I looked with longing eyes to the quiet country where my peasant mother dwelled; but she believed her son was dead. She would not know me in this new shape. I turned towards the city, now deserted by the maddened people.

A wild shout from a thousand throats tore the air. I paused, and looking back, saw that the unchecked vengeance of a generation betrayed by its teachers, had indeed fallen upon the glorious old temple. Already it was desecrated, and its sinful inmates sacrificed. Soon it would be a ruin.

I wandered through the empty streets of the city, and knew that here where I had drunk of pleasure, I must taste the joy of the worker. Here my voice must be heard unceasingly. The truth, long driven from the degraded temple, must find its home in the heart of the people, in the streets of the city. Long time must pass before my sin should fall from me, and leave me stainless, pure, prepared for the perfect life towards which I labor.

Since then, I live, change form, and live again; yet know myself through the long ages as they pass.

Egypt is dead, but her spirit lives, and the knowledge that was hers is still cherished in those souls who have remained true to the grand and mysterious past. They know that out of the profound blindness and inarticulateness of an age of unbelief shall arise the first signs of the splendor of the future. That which is to come is grander, more majestically mysterious than the past. For as the whole life of humanity rises upward, by slow and imperceptible progress, its teachers drink their life from purer founts, and take their message from the soul of existence. The cry has sounded through the world. The truths are uttered in words. Waken dark souls of the earth, who live with eyes upon the ground, raise those dim eyes and let perception enter. Life has in it more than the imagination of man can conceive. Seize boldly upon its mystery, and demand, in the obscure places of your own soul, light with which to illumine those dim recesses of individuality to which you have been blinded through a thousand existences.

Though a land of dusky forms, Egypt stands as a white flower among other races of the earth, and the hieroglyph readers of the old heretic writings, the professors, and the thinkers of the day will be unable to stain the petals of that grand lily blossom of our planet. They do not see the stem of the lily, and the sunlight shining down through the petals. They can see nothing of the real blossom, neither can they disfigure it by modern gardening, because it is out of their reach. It grows above the stature of man and its bulb drinks deep from the river of life.

It flowers in a world of growth to which man can only attain in his absolute moments of inspiration when he is indeed more than man. Therefore, though its lofty stem lifts itself from our world, it is not to be beheld or adequately described, save by one who is in truth so much above the stature of man that he can look down into the face of the flower, wherever it blossoms, whether in the East or the dark West. He will there read the secrets of the controlling forces of the physical plane, and will see, written within it, the science of mystic strength. He will learn how to expound spiritual truths and to enter into the highest self, and he can learn also how to own in life for of that higher self, and yet to retain life upon this planet so long as it shall last, if need be; to retain life in the vigour of manhood, till his entire work is completed, and he has taught the three truths to all who look for light.

Appendices

On *The Idyll of the White Lotus*[1]

Tallapragada Subba Rao

The interesting story published under the title above mentioned has already attracted considerable attention. It is instructive in more ways than one. It truly depicts the Egyptian faith and the Egyptian priesthood, when their religion had already begun to lose its purity and degenerate into a system of Tantric worship contaminated and defiled by black magic, unscrupulously used for selfish and immoral purposes. It is probably also a true story. Sensa is represented to be the last great hierophant of Egypt. Just as a tree leaves its seed to develop into a similar tree, even if it should perish completely, so does every great religion seem to leave its life and energy in one or more great adepts destined to preserve its wisdom and revive its growth at some future time when the cycle of evolution tends in the course of its revolution, to bring about the desired result. The grand old religion of Chemi is destined to reappear on this planet in a higher and nobler form when the appointed time arrives, and there is nothing unreasonable in the supposition that the Sensa of our story is probably now a very high adept, who is waiting to carry out the commands of the Lady of the White Lotus. Apart from these speculations, however, the story in question has a very noble lesson to teach. In its allegorical aspect it describes the trials and

---

1 [First published in Subba Rao 1910:240–252. ME]

the difficulties of a neophyte. It is not easy, however, for the ordinary reader to remove the veil of allegory and clearly understand its teachings. It is to help such readers that I proceed to give the following explanation of the characters that appear in the story in question and the events therein related.

1. *Sensa*, the hero of the story, is intended to represent the human soul. It is the Kūṭastha Caitanyam, or the germ of Prājñā, in which the individuality of the human being is preserved. It corresponds with the higher and permanent element in the 5th principle of man. It is the ego or the self of embodied existence.

2. *Seboua*, the gardener, is *intuition*. "They cannot make a phantom of me," declares Seboua; and in saying so this unsophisticated but honest rustic truly reveals his own mystery.

3. *Agmahd, Kamen-Baka* and the nine other high priests of the temple, who are the devoted servants of the dark goddess whom they worship, represent respectively the following entities:—

    (1) *Kāma* . . . . Desire.
    (2) *Krodha* . . . . Anger.
    (3) *Lobha* . . . . Cupidity.
    (4) *Moha* . . . . Ignorance.
    (5) *Mada* . . . . Arrogance.
    (6) *Matsara* . . . . Jealousy.
    (7, 8, 9, 10, & 11). . . . . The five Senses and
                                      their pleasures.

4. The female characters that figure in the story are the
    following:—

    (1)   The dark and mysterious goddess worshipped
    by the priests;
    (2)   The young girl who played with Sensa;
    (3)   The grown up girl met by him in the City;
    (4)   And lastly, the Lady of the White Lotus.

It must be noticed here that the 2nd and the 3rd are identical. Speaking of the fair woman of the City, whom he met apparently for the first time, Sensa says that as he gazed into her tender eyes it seemed to him that he knew her well and that her charms were familiar to him. It is clear from this statement that this lady is no other than the young girl who ran about the temple with him.

Prakṛti, say the Hindu philosophers, has three qualities, Satva, Rajas, and Tamas. The last of these qualities is connected with the grosser pleasures and passions experienced in Sthūlaśarīra. Rajoguṇa is the cause of the restless activity of the mind, while Satvaguṇa is intimately associated with the spiritual intelligence of man, and with his higher and noble aspirations. Māyā, then, makes its appearance in this story in three distinct forms. It is Vidyā, spiritual intelligence, which is represented by the Lady of the White Lotus. It is the Guānyīn and the Prājñā of the Buddhist writers. She represents the light or the aura of the Logos, which is wisdom, and she is the source of the current of conscious life or Caitanyam. The young girl above referred to is the Mind of man, and it is by her that Sensa is led gradually into the presence of the dark goddess, set up in the holy of the holies for adoration by the priesthood whom we have above described.

The dark goddess herself is *Avidyā*. It is the dark side of human Nature. It derives its life and energy from the passions and desires of the human soul. The ray of life and wisdom, which originally emanated from the Logos and which has acquired a distinct individuality of its own when the process of differentiation has set in, is capable of being transformed more or less entirely into this veritable Kālī, if the light of the Logos is altogether excluded by the bad Karma of the human being, if the voice of intuition is unheard and unnoticed, and if the man lives simply for the purpose of gratifying his own passions and desires.

If these remarks are kept in mind, the meaning of the story will become clear. It is not my object now to write an exhaustive commentary. I shall only notice some of the important incidents and their significance.

Look upon Sensa as a human being, who, after running his course through several incarnations, and after having passed through a considerable amount of spiritual training, is born again in this world with his spiritual powers of perception greatly developed, and prepared to become a neophyte at a very early stage in his career. As soon as he enters into the physical body, he is placed under the charge of the five Senses and the six Emotions above enumerated, who have it as their place of residence. The human Soul is first placed under the guidance of his own intuition, the simple and honest gardener of the temple, for whom the High Priests seem to have no respect or affection, and, when it has not yet lost its original purity, gets a glimpse of its spiritual intelligence, the Lady of the White Lotus. The priests, however, are determined that no opportunity should be given for the intuition to work, and they there-fore remove the child from its guardianship and introduce him to their own dark goddess, the goddess of human passion. The very sight of this deity is found repulsive to the human soul at first. The proposed transfer of human consciousness and human attachment from the spiritual plane to the physical plane is too abrupt and premature to succeed. The priests failed in their first attempt and began to devise their plans for a second effort in the same direction.

Before proceeding further I must draw the reader's attention to the real meaning of the Lotus tank in the garden Sahasrāra Cakra in the brain is often spoken of as a Lotus Tank in the Hindu mystical books. The "sweet sounding water" of this tank is described as Amṛtam or nectar. See p. 349 of the second volume of *Isis Unveiled* for further hints as regards the meaning of this magic water. Padma, the White Lotus, is said to have a thousand petals, as has the mysterious Sahasrāram of the Yogis. It is an unopened bud in the ordinary mortal, and just as a lotus opens its petals, and expand in all its bloom and beauty when the sun rises above the horizon and sheds his rays on the flower, so does the Sahasrāram of the neophyte open and expand when the Logos begins to pour its light into its centre. When fully expanded it becomes the glorious seat of the Lady of the Lotus, the sixth principle of man; and sitting on this flower the great goddess pours out the waters of life and grace for the gratification and the regeneration of the human soul.

Haṭha Yogis say that the human soul in *Samādhi* ascends to this thousand-petalled flower through Suṣumṇa (the *Da'at* of the Kabbalists) and obtains a glimpse of the splendour of the spiritual sun.

In this part of Sensa's life an event is related which deserves attention. An elemental appearing in the guise of a neophyte of the temple tries to take him out from his physical body. This is a danger to which a man is liable before he acquires sufficient proficiency as an adept to guard himself against all such dangers, especially when his internal perception is developed to a certain extent. Sensa's guardian angel protects him from the danger owing to his innocence and purity.

When the mental activity of the child commences and absorbs its attention, it recedes farther and farther from the Light of the Logos. Its intuition will not be in a position to work unshackled. Its suggestions come to it mixed up with other states of consciousness which are the result of sensation and intellection. Unable to see Sensa and speak to him personally, Seboua sends him his beloved lotus flower surreptitiously through one of the neophytes of the temple.

Mental activity commences first by way of sensation. Emotions make their appearance subsequently. The opening mind of the child is aptly compared to a little girl playing with Sensa. When once the mind begins to exercise its functions the pleasures of sensation soon pave the way for the strong and fierce emotions of the human soul. Sensa has descended one step from the spiritual plane when he loses sight of the sublime lotus flower and its glorious goddess and begins to be amused by the frolicsome little girl. "You are to live among Earth-fed flower," says this little girl to him, disclosing the change that has already taken place. At first it is the simple beauty of nature that engrosses the attention of Sensa. But his mind soon leads him to the dark goddess of the shrine. Avidyā has its real seat in mind, and it is impossible to resist its influence so long as the mind of man is not restrained in its action. When once the soul gets under the influence of this dark goddess, the high priests of the temple begin to utilize its powers for their own benefit and gratification. The goddess requires twelve priests in all, including Sensa, to help her cause. Unless the six emotions and the five sensations above enumerated are banded together she cannot exercise her sway completely. They support and strengthen each other as every man's experience clearly demonstrates. Isolated, they are weak and can easily be subdued, but when associated together their combined power is strong enough to keep the soul under control. The fall of Sensa now becomes complete, but not before he receives a well merited rebuke from the gardener and a word of warning from the Lady of the Lotus.

Addressing Sensa, Seboua is made to utter the following words: "You came first to work; you were to be the drudge for me; now all is changed. Yon are to play, not work, and I am to treat you like a little prince. Well! Have they spoiled thee yet, I wonder, child?" These words are significant; and their meaning will become plain by the light of the foregoing remarks. It must be noted that the last time he went into the garden, Sensa was taken, not to the Lotus Tank, but to another tank receiving its waters from the former.

Owing to the change that has come over him, Sensa is unable to see the Light of the Logos by direct perception, but is under the necessity of recognizing the same by the operation of his fifth principle. It is in the astral fluid that he floats and not in the magic water of the Lotus Tank. He sees, nevertheless, the Lady of the Lotus who pathetically says, "Soon thou wilt leave me; and how can I aid thee if thou forgettest me utterly?"

After this occurrence Sensa becomes completely a man of the world, living for the pleasures of the physical life. His developed mind becomes his companion and the priest of the temple profit by the change. Before proceeding further I must draw the reader's attention to the possibility of eliciting from a child any desired information by invoking certain elementals and other powers, by means of magic rites and ceremonies. After the soul gets completely under the influence of Avidyā, it may either succumb altogether to the said influence, and get absorbed, as it were, in the Tamoguṇa of Prakṛti, or dispel its own ignorance by the light of spiritual wisdom and shake off this baneful influence. A critical moment arrives in the history of Sensa when his very existence is merged up for the time being with the dark goddess of human passion on the day of the boat festival. Such an absorption, however short, is the first step towards final extinction. He must either be saved at this critical juncture or perish. The Lady of the White Lotus, his guardian angel, makes a final attempt to save him, and succeeds. In the very holy of the holies, she unveils the dark goddess; and Sensa, perceiving his folly prays for deliverance from the accursed yoke of the hated priesthood. His prayer is granted, and relying upon the support of the bright goddess he revolts against the authority of the priests, and directs the attention of the people to the iniquities of the temple authorities.

It is necessary to say a few words in this connection as regards the real nature of soul-death and the ultimate fate of a black magician, to impress the teachings of this book on the mind of the reader. The soul, as we have above explained, is an isolated drop in the ocean of cosmic life. This current of cosmic life is but the light and the aura of the Logos. Besides the Logos, there are innumerable other existences, both spiritual and astral, partaking of this life and living in it. These beings have special affinities with particular emotions of the human soul and particular characteristics of the human mind. They have of course a definite individual existence of their own which lasts up to the end of the Manvantara. There are three ways in which a soul may cease to retain its special individuality. Separated from its Logos, which is, as it were, its source, it may not acquire a strong and abiding individuality of its own, and may in course of time be reabsorbed into the current of Universal Life. This is real soul-death. It may also place itself *en rapport* with a spiritual or elemental existence by evoking it, and concentrating its attention and regard on it for purposes of black magic and Tantric worship. In such a case it transfers its individuality to such existence and is sucked up into it, as it were. In such a case the black magician lives in such a being, and as such a being he continues till the end of Manvantara.

The fate of Banasena illustrates the point. After his death he is said to live as Mahākāla, one of the most powerful spirits of Pramathagana. In some respects this amounts to acquiring immortality in evil. But unlike the immortality of the Logos it does not go beyond Manvantaric limits. Read the 8th chapter of Bhagavad Gita in this connection, and my meaning will become clear by the light of Kṛṣṇa's teaching. The occurrence in the boat of Isis, depicted in the book under consideration, gives some idea of the nature of this absorption and the subsequent preservation of the magician's individuality.

When the centre of absorption is the Logos and not any other power or elemental, the man acquires Mukti or Nirvāṇa and becomes one with the eternal Logos without any necessity of rebirth.

The last part of the book describes the final struggle of the soul with its inveterate foes, its initiation and ultimate deliverance from the tyranny of Prakṛti.

The assurance and the advice given by the Lady of the White Lotus to Sensa in the holy of holies marks the great turning point in the history of his career. He has perceived the light of the Divine Wisdom and has brought himself within the pale of its influence. This light of the Logos, which is represented in the story as the fair goddess of the sacred flower of Egypt, is the bond of union and brother-hood which maintains the chain of spiritual intercourse and sympathy running through the long succession of the great hierophants of Egypt, and extending to all the great adepts of this world who derive their influx of spiritual life from the same source. It is the Holy Ghost that keeps up the apostolical succession or Guruparaṃparā as the Hindus call it. It is this spiritual light which is transmitted from Guru to disciple when the time of real initiation comes. The so-called "transfer of life" is no other than the transmission of this light. And further, the Holy Ghost, which is, as it were, the veil or the body of the Logos and hence its flesh and blood, is the basis of the holy communion. Every fraternity of adepts has this bond of union; and time and space cannot tear it asunder. Even when there is an apparent break in the succession on the physical plane, a neophyte following the sacred law and aspiring towards a higher life, will not be in want of guidance and advice when the proper time arrives, though the last Guru may have died several thousands of years before he was born. Every Buddha meets at his last initiation all the great adepts who reached Buddhahood during the preceding ages: and similarly every class of adepts has its own bond of spiritual communion which knits them together into a properly organized fraternity. The only possible and effectual way of entering into any such brotherhood, or partaking of the holy communion, is by bringing oneself within the influence of the spiritual light which radiates from one's own Logos. I may further point out here, without venturing to enter into details, that such communion is only possible between persons whose souls derive their life and sustenance from the same divine ray, and that, as seven distinct rays radiate from the "Central Spiritual Sun", all adepts and Dhyan Chohans are divisible into seven classes, each of which is guided, controlled and overshadowed by one of seven forms or manifestations of the divine wisdom.

In this connection it is necessary to draw the reader's attention to another general law which regulates the circulation of spiritual life and energy through the several adepts who belong to the same fraternity. Each adept may be conceived as a centre wherein this spiritual force is generated and stored up, and through which it is utilized and distributed. This mysterious energy is a kind of spiritual electrical force, and its transmission from one centre to another presents some of the phenomena noticed in connection with electrical induction. Consequently there is a tendency towards the equalization of the amounts of energy stored up in the various centres. The quantity of the neutral fluid existing in any particular centre depends upon the man's Karma and the holiness and purity of his life. When evoked into activity by being brought into communication with his Guru or Initiator it becomes dynamic, and has a tendency to transfer itself to weaker centres. It is sometimes stated that, at the time of the final initiation, either the hierophant or the "newly born," the *worthier* of the two must die (see page 38, *Theosophist*, November 1882). Whatever may be the real nature of this mysterious death, it is due to the operation of this law. It will be further seen that a new initiate, if he is weak in spiritual energy, is strengthened by partaking of the holy communion; and for obtaining this advantage he has to remain on earth and utilize his power for the good of mankind until the time of final liberation arrives. This is an arrangement which harmonizes with the Law of Karma. The neophyte's original weakness is due to his Karmic defects. These defects necessitate a longer period of physical existence. And this period he will have to spend in the cause of human progress in return for the benefit above indicated. And, moreover, the accumulated good Karma of this period has the effect of strengthening his soul, and when he finally takes his place in the Sacred Brotherhood, he brings as much spiritual capital with him as any of the others for carrying on the work of the said fraternity.

If these few remarks are borne in mind, the incidents related in the last five chapters will soon disclose their real significance. When Sensa gains his power of spiritual perception through the grace of his guardian angel, and begins to exercise it knowingly and voluntarily, he has no occasion to rely on the flickering light of intuition. "You must now stand alone," says the gardener, and places him in possession of his beloved flower, the full meaning of which Sensa begins to understand. Having thus gained the seat of spiritual clairvoyance, Sensa perceives the hierophants who preceded him and into whose fraternity he has entered. The Guru is always ready when the disciple is ready. The initiation preceding the final struggle for liberty from the bondage of matter is pretty plainly described. The highest Chohan reveals to him the secrets of occult science, and another adept of the Brotherhood points out to him the real basis and nature of his own personality. His immediate predecessor then comes to his assistance and reveals to him the mystery of his own Logos. "The veil of Isis" is removed, White Lotus, his real Saviour, lay concealed. The Light of the Logos enters his soul and he is made to pass through the "baptism by Divine Fire". He hears the final directions given by his Queen and recognises the duty cast upon his shoulders.

His predecessor, whose soul is so "white and spotless", is commanded to give him a portion of his spiritual strength and energy. The three great truths which underlie every religion, however, disfigured and distorted, through ignorance, superstition and prejudice, are then taught to him for the purpose of being proclaimed to the world at large. It is needless for me to explain these truths here as their enunciation in the book is sufficiently plain. Thus fortified and instructed Sensa prepares for the final struggle. During these preparatory stages the passions of the physical man are, as it were, dormant, and Sensa is left alone for the time being. But they are not entirely subdued. The decisive battle is yet to be fought and won. Sensa begins to enter on the higher spiritual life as a preacher and spiritual guide to men, directed by the light of wisdom which has entered his soul. But he cannot pursue this course for any length of time before be has conquered his foes. The moment for the final struggle of the last initiation soon arrives. The nature of this initiation is very little understood. It is sometimes represented in vague terms as a terrible ordeal through which an initiate has to pass before he becomes a real adept. It is further characterized as "the baptism by blood." These general statements do not in the least indicate the precise nature of the result to be achieved by the neophyte or the difficulties he has to encounter.

It is necessary to enquire into the nature of the psychic change or transformation which is intended to be effected by this initiation before its mystery is understood. According to the ordinary Vedantic classification there are four states of conscious existence, *viz.*, *Viśva*, *Taijasa*, *Prājñā*, and *Turīya*. In modern language these may be described as the objective, the clairvoyant, the ecstatic, and the ultra-ecstatic states of consciousness. The seats or *upadhis* related to these conditions are the physical body, the astral body, the *Kāraṇaśarīra* or the Monad and the Logos. The soul is the Monad. It is, as it were, the neutral point of consciousness. It is germ of *prājñā*. When completely isolated no consciousness is experienced by it. Its psychic condition is hence compared by Hindu writers to *Suṣupti*—a condition of dreamless sleep. But it is under the influence of the physical body and the astral body on the one side, and the sixth and seventh principles on the other. When the attraction of the former prevails, the *Jīva* becomes *Buddha* and is subject to all the passions of embodied existence. The power of these passions grows weaker and weaker as the neutral point we have indicated is approached. But so long as the neutral barrier is not crossed their attraction is felt. But when once this is effected, the soul is, as it were, placed under the control and attraction of the other pole—the Logos; and the man becomes liberated from the bondage of matter. In short he becomes an adept. The struggle for supremacy between these two forces of attraction takes place on this neutral barrier. But during the struggle the person in whose interest the battle is fought is in a quiescent, unconscious condition, almost helpless to assist his friends or strike hard at his enemies, though the result of the fight is a matter of life and death to him. This is the condition in which Sensa finds himself in passing through the last ordeal, and the description of the said condition in the book under examination becomes clear by the light of the foregoing explanations. It can be easily seen that the result of the fight will mainly depend upon the *latent* energy of the soul, its previous training and its past Karma. But our hero passes successfully through the ordeal; his enemies are completely overthrown. But *Sensa* dies in the struggle.

Strangely enough when the enemy is defeated, the *Personality* of Sensa is destroyed on the field of battle. This is the final sacrifice which he makes, and his mother, *Prakṛti*—the mother of his personality—laments his loss, but rejoices at the prospect of the resurrection of his soul. The resurrection soon takes place; his soul rises from the grave as it were, under the vivifying influence of his spiritual intelligence, to shed its blessings on mankind and work for the spiritual development of his fellow beings. Here ends the so-called tragedy of the soul. What follows is merely intended to bring the story in its quasi-historical aspect to a proper conclusion.

The Story of Sensa

The Story of Sensa[1]
An Interpretation of The Idyll of the White Lotus

Mabel Collins

The interesting story published under the title above mentioned has already attracted considerable attention. It is instructive in more ways than one. It truly depicts the Egyptian faith and the Egyptian priesthood, when their religion had already begun to lose its purity and degenerate into a system of Tantric worship contaminated and defiled by black magic, unscrupulously used for selfish and immoral purposes. It is probably also a true story. Sensa is represented to be the last great hierophant of Egypt. Just as a tree leaves its seed to develop into a similar tree, even if it should perish completely, so does every great religion seem to leave its life and energy in one or more great adepts destined to preserve its wisdom and revive its growth at some future time when the cycle of evolution tends in the course of its revolution, to bring about the desired result. The grand old religion of Chemi is destined to reappear on this planet in a higher and nobler form when the appointed time arrives, and there is nothing unreasonable in the supposition that the Sensa of our story is probably now a very high adept, who is waiting to carry out the commands of the Lady of the White Lotus. Apart from these specula-

---

1   [First published as a monograph in 1913 by John W. Lovell, New York. ME]

tions, however, the story in question has a very noble lesson to teach. In its allegorical aspect it describes the trials and the difficulties of a neophyte. It is not easy, however, for the ordinary reader to remove the veil of allegory and clearly understand its teachings. It is to help such readers that I proceed to give the following explanation of the characters that appear in the story in question and the events therein related.

Chapter I

The story of Sensa, as told with marvellous and mystic art in *The Idyll of the White Lotus* contains within itself three narratives, separate yet inseparable, united in their very nature and essence, as are the three leaflets of the trefoil clover. They cannot be taken apart, but they can be looked upon separately and in each is contained something vital which appeals to the deepest part of the human nature within ourselves. No student of occultism who has once read this Idyll and penetrated within any part of its mystic veil, can forget it or be parted from it, because it relates his own story, the tragedy and ultimate apotheosis of his own soul, and is therefore an essential part of himself.

I am able to write of *The Idyll* as a critic and a student, not as its author in any sense, because I simply placed it upon paper in human language, as it was told to me in the mystical and universal language, when my personality was in the state known to the occultists of Southern India as "svapna"—obscurely translated into English by the words "somnambulic clairvoyance". In 1878 I was deeply engrossed in literary work which kept me constantly at my writing table, and from the window of the room I worked in I saw Cleopatra's Needle brought up the river and set up upon the Embankment. A procession of superb Egyptian priests began from that time to come into my room—coming up the staircase and entering the door—

and stood around my table. I thought at first it was the appearance of astral forms connected with the Needle. But as these mysterious visits continued and culminated in a great effort, it is evident that if they were astral forms they were animated and directed by the egos to which they belonged, and were indeed the Kas of certain priests of ancient Egypt. It is of course known as a fact that the religious Egyptians understood that the Ka or astral form of a person who had lived a spiritual life could be used by the ego of that person for great purposes if carefully preserved and protected. Also it has been stated that the Ka or astral form exists to serve the purpose of supplying information with regard to events on the physical plane to its ego in Devachan. This seems to be what took place in this case, and when the hour was ripe the ego came to the place where its work had to be done, and aroused the ego within myself so that I stood out of myself to receive the message, and wrote it down upon the paper on my table, arresting the thinking principle of my brain in its action while this was accomplished. Thus the story was passed from the higher consciousness to the lower, intact and perfect. The "Ka" of the Ancient Egyptians is the "astral form" of the Theosophists, the "spook" of the spiritualist's seance room, the "ghost" of all time and all countries. It was regarded by the Egyptians as earthbound, unenlightened, ignorant and retaining the lowest of the physical desires of the man. They had an object in keeping it imprisoned in the tomb of the body, and they therefore provided it with amusements and pleasures there to prevent its roaming about and perhaps seeking still less desirable gratifications. They had an elaborate ritual by which they kept it there instead of allowing it to become disintegrated on the astral plane. This was done because they held that the ego in its high place might in the future need its services upon earth, and come to seek it; and they believed that from time to time this occurred. Of course the priests's knowledge of magic and the mysteries of the after life was regarded as great enough to establish and hold such a connection over the centuries. The shapes of priests who came into my room and stood around my table before *The Idyll of the White Lotus* was written were not seen by others; it required "waking clairvoyance" (*jāgrat*) to perceive them; but still, they were ghosts, pure and simple, the shades of the dead. But, as no doubt the ego of a great adept undertook the task of writing *The Idyll* it is more than probable that at the moment when the work was actually begun, when I was summoned into the higher consciousness, each one of these ghosts was inhabited by its true ego, or spiritual form.

These priests were not the priests who appear as characters in the book; it is necessary to state this clearly to avoid any confusion. The priests who gave the story of Sensa to the world were representatives of the great spiritual religion, (that " white magic " which came from prehistoric times,) acting once more in a definite manner upon man and aiding his evolution.

The priests in the story represent those who were sorcerers, workers of "black magic".

It must be remembered that magic is a word of dignity and spirituality, derived as it is, from the ancient Zend. It simply means the powers and practices of the wise men, the Magi. Professor Wallis Budge says: "The belief in magic, the word being used in its best sense, is older in Egypt than the belief in God."[2]—"Egyptian magic dates from the time when the pre-dynastic and prehistoric dwellers in Egypt believed that [the earth, and the

---

2 [Budge 1901:ix. ME]

underworld, and the] air, and the sky were peopled with countless beings, visible and invisible, which were held to be friendly or unfriendly to man—"[3] He points out that the magic known in other countries has been drawn from "the White Magic" and "the Black Magic" of ancient Egypt, and adds: "it is impossible to say exactly how much the beliefs and religious systems of other nations were influenced by them, but there is no doubt that certain views and religious ideas of many heathen and Christian sects may be traced directly to them."

This is the glorious side of the retrospect, showing how the highest that is in us, and the best that we know, has its origin and root in the mysterious prehistoric past of Egypt.

A great, dark, gloomy shape arises from the same ancient source and the light and the darkness battled ceaselessly then as they have done ever since, in the world and in every man's own nature.

Professor Wallis Budge says:

> To him that was versed in the lore contained 8 in the books of 'the double house of life' the future was as well known as the past and neither time nor distance could limit the operations of his power; the mysteries of life and death were laid bare before him—Now if such views as these concerning the magician's power were held by the educated folk of ancient Egypt there is little to wonder at when we find that beliefs and superstitions of the most degraded character flourished with rank luxuriance among the peasants and working classes of that country—To meet the religious needs of such people the magician, and in later times the priest,

---

3   [Budge 1901:viii. The phrase in square brackets was transposed in error in *The Story of Sensa* and appeared between "unfriendly" and "to man". ME]

found it necessary to provide pageants and ceremonies which appealed chiefly to the senses—this magic degenerated into sorcery, and demonology, and witchcraft, and those who dealt in it were regarded as associates of the Devil and servants of the powers of darkness, and workers of the "black art".

Here we have the atmosphere in which the story of Sensa is set, we feel how true to life is the picture of the innocent neophyte plunged into the battle between the powers of good and evil. Subba Rao, the learned Brahmin Theosophist says of *The Idyll*:[4]

It truly depicts the Egyptian faith and the Egyptian priesthood, when their religion had already begun to lose its purity and degenerate into a system of Tantric worship contaminated and defiled by black magic, unscrupulously used for selfish and immoral purposes.

If we first of all read *The Idyll* in its artistic setting as a story of ancient Egypt, laid in one of its great Temples, (now long since a ruin, buried beneath the dust of ages,) we see the young boy, born of the peasants, a fellah, chosen out of his family to enter its sacred hidden priestly life as a novice. He is innocent, untrained, simple. He is awestruck at the vocation open to him, and at the majesty and dignity of the priests. To them he is simply an ignorant boy from the country who will have enough work given him to do, such as he is fitted for. They think nothing of him, and Agmahd, the high priest of the "dark goddess", the leader of the group of black magicians, does

---

4   Subba Rao 1910:240. [See p. 121 above. ME]

not notice how profound is the impression made on the sensitive child by his presence and personality. His golden beard, his exquisite robe, white, embroidered with gold in mystic patterns, the glamour which encompassed him, filled Sensa with strange new emotions, inexplicable and bewildering. In spite of his charm and gentleness the child recognized in him something hard and cold, something scarcely human. He indicates this by saying that Agmahd seemed to him like something carved. Agmahd sees a timid boy, and bids him not to fear. He directs that he shall be taken into the school. Here where pale students study difficult papyri, the priest who is their teacher treats him with contempt. The new novice is only a country boy, clearly no scholar; there is no time to be wasted on him. He directs that the child be taken to the gardener, who will be able to give him some work. He goes into this place of beauty, and being a seer and clairvoyant becomes aware of the presence of The Goddess—the spirit of true religion becomes visible to him, personified, rising out of the sacred flower of Egypt. In full waking clairvoyance he gazes upon her, and then tries to approach her, but this effort is too great, and he faints away.

The fact that he is a seer at once changes his position in the Temple. The black magicians determine to control him and use his gifts for their own ends. They are in great need of one with this gift, to act as a medium for their dark goddess, to enable her to communicate with them and with the people. Every effort is made to secure him for this purpose. The battle between the two forces of good and evil literally rage over him. He is of priceless value to Agmahd and the black magicians who follow and obey him. They have need of a medium, there is no seer or clairvoyant amongst them, and although they have all the learning of the ancient Egyptian, all the powers of the students of magic, they cannot communicate with their innermost guide and controller, the dark Queen, without the psychic gift. It has been lost by reason of their utter selfishness and degradation, so that they have had nothing to offer the people but inventions and deceit. They are placed before us in the position of the fortunetellers and miracle-workers of to-day—when the power has left them, in order to keep the suffrages and the support of the public on whom they depend it becomes necessary to invent and to lie. The company of the high priests are weary of subterfuge and exhausted in invention. The discovery of a natural clairvoyant, a born seer, in one of the young neophytes, is to them like the sight of gold in the soil to a gold-digger. The child must be secured, made their slave, trained in mediumship, taught how to listen to the strange voice of the dark Queen (the personification of evil and falsehood and selfishness, and to give her messages to her servants; taught how to take their requests to her and obtain from her the gratification of their desires. This is the vocation laid down for Sensa, upon which he is to enter immediately, without any delay whatever. They cannot afford to wait—they have sold their very souls to the Devil, and they must have payment—power and the gratification of desire for themselves, miracles and excitement for the people who support them. None of these things can they get, because there is none among them with psychic power, none who is not bound by materialism in consequence of evil doing and selfishness. Therefore so soon as the gardener tells them that the child has seen a vision, they claim him for their own. But the vision was that of Truth, of the personification of the Logos; the Lily-Queen of Egypt's pure religion had discovered his open sight before the black magicians knew of it; and his heart had gone out to truth and purity and love; he had done obeisance to the Supreme. Therefore the black magicians found the task of subduing him to their evil purposes, and selfish will, much harder than they had expected it to be. They thought he was merely an ignorant boy who would be as wax in their hands; whom they could use and exploit without difficulty; but he was indeed a human being within whom was illumination and who was struggling to retain it and to draw nearer and nearer to the light. The ordeals to which he was subjected, the temptations placed in his way, the seductions offered to him, give the setting of sombre and brilliant pictures required for the enactment of this tragedy of the soul.

That the black magicians should have so misjudged the neophyte is perfectly natural and true to life. An inability to recognise the higher natures is a characteristic of those who have chosen the path of self -aggrandisement. The priests who surrounded Sensa were so deeply plunged in the gratification of desire and in the blind materialism which results from it, that they no longer understood the laws of evolution and did not realise that waking clairvoyance and the true Vision are only possible to one who has entered upon the upward path. Therefore they miscalculated his strength, and met with a resistance they did not look for. They thought that by the mere exercise of authority over this helpless child they could get all that they wanted. And at first it seemed as if it was to be so. He was taken into the holy of holies in which dwelled the dark Power. Again he sees—this time to tremble with horror. And he refuses to obey the command of the dark Power; fainting, once more, from exhaustion. And so passed his first day within the Temple. The priests seek for means to entice the soul from the body, and leave it uncontrolled, to be used by the dark Queen as her medium; the attempts in which the fascinations and pleasures of black magic on the subtle planes of experience are offered to him seems at first to be successful. The longing for freedom from his imprisonment can be gratified by leaving his body; and when the chance to do this comes he takes it without hesitation, in complete ignorance of the danger. But the Lotus Queen herself comes to his entranced body and wakens it and calls the soul back to take the command. Then Agmahd creates a personification of pleasure, which comes to the boy as another child, a girl full of fun and play. This most difficult feat of the black magician brings success at last; Sensa follows his new playmate with natural delight. She leads him into gardens of flowers; among children who are playing games; and he becomes possessed by the very spirit of pleasure, playing eagerly with the others. This time Agmahd conquered; while the soul wandered away into the world of childlike delights, the entranced body was seized upon, used, controlled by the dark Goddess. The *soul of the neophyte* saw itself surrounded by merry children like himself; the *body of the neophyte* was raised up and surrounded by worshipping priests, its voice used to utter words of authority. The gay and innocent soul which had been led from one plane to another by Agmahd's magical powers was happy in the experiences of dream-consciousness, while its body was thus used. Returning to its own place it found all changed. No longer was the ego of this neophyte the ruler of its body. The boy had become a medium, made so by witchcraft and sorcery despite the power of the Lotus Queen. His voice had been used without his knowledge. His body had been worshipped as the dwelling and vehicle of the *Avidyā* herself while he had been playing with his child friends in the dream consciousness. It is a most interesting study in the simultaneous enactment of events, and in the passing of the soul from one state of consciousness to another, which is here given. Ambition and emulation have come to him in the subtile consciousness, artfully drawn forth in him by the black magician who is guiding his fate; he is the successful competitor in the games, and then he is lifted up to be a leader of the children and placed on a throne in their midst to speak to them. He is quite forgetful of his body and of his responsibility with regard to it, excited by the subtile pleasures offered to him. Then he "fell asleep" as it is expressed. Any one who has had a very vivid dream consciousness and returned suddenly from it to the physical consciousness will recognise this description as' perfectly correct. The feeling is exactly the same as that of falling asleep in the physical consciousness. Followed by the voices of the children acclaiming him and praising him, he entered into his body and found it surrounded by worshipping priests to whom he had spoken words he knew not, and could not have understood if he had known them. The only child among the crowd was the little girl who had led him into the gardens of subtile pleasure and returned with him; the creature of Agmahd, a form animated by his mind. The manner in which this child appears, and her actions, is one of the signs of that high priest being a very highly advanced Yogin, a *sorcerer* of the first rank. And even now, so late in his career, he might have cast the darkness from him and become by suffering and expiation, a *Yogin* of the first rank. But he is unable to pass beyond the contemplation of the phenomenal universe. He cannot escape from the thrall of the dominating characteristic of his nature, the love of power. He is destroyed by his own ambition. He has conquered the child-seer who goes helplessly with him into the desecrated and terrible Holy of Holies, there to be the medium between him and his evil ruler. He has sought long for this opportunity of direct communication with the powerful spirit, determined to secure the prizes for which he has worked, the gratification of his colossal ambition. He desires to be a ruler in the world of men, to wear a crown of absolute power. Now he is able, by reason of his conquest of Sensa's will, to make his final demand of the evil one. And he is immediately confronted by the supreme ordeal of the black magician. Till now he has retained his claim to immortality and to the possibility of ultimate redemption. But if he is to have his desired prize, he must surrender the heritage of man. he must sell his birthright. And after a brief pause, in which his great intellect and his widely developed consciousness, survey the bargain, he pronounces "the fatal words". Henceforth he is one of the *Prakṛtilaya*, those Yogins who are soulless and without knowledge of the Supreme, and who must ultimately be disintegrated, or "resolved into nature" because there is no spiritual being within which can live on. And the boy, looking on him as he makes the dreadful choice, sees that his face grows "colder and more stony than any carven form". Already he experiences an augmentation of the peculiar strength of the magician. He exhibits the complete perfection of body which is one of the powers of the magician, the perfection which according to Patañjali, the Persian sage, includes "beauty, gracefulness, strength, and adamantine hardness". The aspect as of a carved figure had belonged to him in the eyes of the child-seer from the first; now it has become confirmed. Agmahd has bartered immortality for a mortality during which he can be injured by none, he can suffer no ill, he will be immune from all danger. Such are the great and terrible beings who appear as rulers of masses of men from time to time, who conquer and control by sheer force of will, who bear charmed lives, against whom revenge and justice are alike unavailing.

In order to give to Agmahd the crown which he demands of her the evil spirit requires twelve "sworn servants" to do her bidding. For there is work to do, and the workers must be secured. The dark Queen tells Agmahd that the number must be complete. There are ten priests in the Temple who are hungry with desire for pleasure; the dark Queen promises to satisfy them and in so doing to bind them to their service. There is Kamen Baka, the second in dignity in the Temple; his heart's desire is known to the dark Queen and she is prepared to gratify it, without delay. "And who shall be the one to complete the number?" asks Agmahd.

"This child," she answers, and by those words the fate of Sensa is sealed; that fate which changes him from "a gay child, a happy creature of sunshine" into a "sad youth" whose "sick heart held hidden within it many secrets" of shame and sin and sorrow, and who knew himself for a slave.

This terrible scene is immediately followed by the summons from the dark Queen to Kamen Baka. He enters the holy of holies, a blind man, stumbling in the dark, seeing nothing, altogether dependent on the mediumship of another, despised by the evil power whom he serves. The dark Queen views him with contempt because his human personality is his limitation. He craves personal adoration, personal love given to him by those around him, whom he feels regard him now with coldness and dislike. His demand is easily granted, if he pronounces the fatal words which belong to this step in the downward path. He knows well what they are, and with the dreadful glare upon his face of the one who desires to have and to take all and give nothing, utters them, though with pain. "From henceforward, though all men love me, I love no man."

The dark Queen knows that the strength of the young seer has been tried to the uttermost, and orders that he shall be given rest. Agmahd therefore leaves him to himself and tells the gardener to take him out among the flowers. Seboua is not to take him to the lotus tank but among beautiful things which refresh his soul and awaken his artistic nature. But all true art is fed from the Supreme, and in the midst of his delight in beauty, of his rejoicing in the glory of life, the Lady of the Lotus suddenly comes to him and tells him the mystery of the water, and shows him how to rise upon it. But he is not strong enough to remain with her; he falls away, sinking back into the darkness of his slavery and the words she speaks to him become but a memory. But still he cherishes them in his heart and they ring out dimly from time to time in the obscure regions of his darkened brain, as the years of slavery and shame pass by and he grows, in his bondage, from childhood to manhood. So ends the first Book of *The Idyll*. The battle for this poor human soul still rages, the Supreme holds fast to the spark of divinity which it has lit, though apparently Sensa is lost and is fated to be one of the black magicians.

Chapter II

The first book of *The Idyll* can be read as the story of any neophyte of the priesthood in the days of the degeneracy and degradation of the great religion of Egypt, if he was found to be a natural psychic. But the second book contains scenes and events which show that Sensa regarded as an individual, was not only a seer but a soul so highly advanced as to be ready to become an adept. He is moreover described as a hierophant, one who teaches. So that in reading the detailed description of the ordeals and tests through which he passes, it is inevitable that the student of occultism shall look upon him as a recognized personality, one of the great ones of the race. Subba Rao, who observes[5] that *The Idyll* is probably a true story, goes on to say,

> Sensa is represented to be the last great hierophant of Egypt. Just as a tree leaves its seed to develop into a similar tree, even if it should perish completely, so does every great religion seem to leave its life and energy in one or more great adepts destined to preserve its wisdom and revive its growth at some future time when the cycle of evolution tends in the course of its revolution, to bring about the desired result. The grand old religion of Chemi is destined to reappear on this

5   Subba Rao 1910:240. [See p. 121 above. ME]

planet in a higher and nobler form when the appointed time arrives, and there is nothing unreasonable in the supposition that the Sensa of our story is probably now a very high adept, who is waiting to carry out the commands of the Lady of the White Lotus.

This view, of course, is based upon the character of the ordeals described, and upon Sensa's action in teaching the people. The grounds for it are inherent in the story. But it is not possible to identify Sensa with any known adept, nor has any such attempt been made except as a vague speculation. Still, the idea suggested by Subba Rao that the ego of Sensa may yet have service to do for humanity gives a keen interest to the character and adds to the profound occultism of the story the romance of a personal touch. The Sensa of whose trials and fierce struggles we read may be amongst us now—visible or invisible—embodied or unembodied.

In the beginning of the second book we are shown the boy grown to manhood, though still a young man. He is valued and cared for in the Temple as such a priceless servant would be; he is amused and waited upon by other young priests in the intervals of the exhausting forms of mediumship to which he is compelled to give himself. The waking clairvoyance in which, in his more innocent days, he became conscious of the Lady of the Lotus and received her direct inspiration, has apparently become no longer possible for him. He is utterly given over to the madness of irresponsible mediumship, and knows nothing of the dread teachings and instructions uttered in his voice to the priestly sorcerers. He needs not only rest but refreshment to preserve his vitality. The dark goddess had said to him in his childhood that he must have beauty. She told him that he would have been a great artist if he had lived for beauty; but that might not be. He had other work to do. In his childhood and youth he was surrounded with quantities of flowers and all beautiful things; as he grew to manhood he needed more than this, and was allowed to go out of the Temple into the city and find pleasures that would restore his strength. Throughout the story he is shown as being only attracted by beauty, or by pleasures of a beautiful kind. He had felt no interest in any of the mental work or mental studies done in the Temple; this would naturally be the case with a child-seer, and regarding the story as that of one who was passing through the initiations of adeptship, it is evident that he would have evolved beyond the mental plane. But beauty and beautiful pleasures attracted him so deeply that this was indeed his undoing. By recognizing and taking advantage of this part of his nature Agmahd had obtained control over him at the beginning. And now the slave of the high priest was sent out to experience all the seductions and passions of human life in the city; knowing full well that his chains were upon him and that when his strength was restored he would be recalled. It is at this point in the story that a new character appears, Malen, a young priest who is his companion, whose connection with him is full of mystery and meaning. It is Malen who suggests to him to go forth in search of pleasure, as otherwise he will die of exhaustion; and who assures him that Agmahd has already given permission. Malen leads him forth and leaves him in the city with a beautiful woman who is evidently a re-appearance of the personification of pleasure known to him in childhood as his little girl playmate. The description of his meeting with her again is most wonderfully vivid. He is amazed to think that he has so long neglected her. So Malen leaves him in the company of a creature formed by Agmahd from one of the serpents which are the dark Queen's living robe. When the child-seer's innocent eyes had seen this garment of Desire upon the evil spirit it had filled him with horror. But this horror had left him, he had become familiar with the aspect of the monstrous forms; and now when by sorcery the evil thing was made lovely he dwelled with it in delight. Uncounted Time passed by; he reckoned it not. But Agmahd watched and waited, counting all and knowing all. And when the great day of the river festival arrived he went into the city of pleasure to fetch the seer of the Temple, saying simply: "Come!" And the seer, knowing himself a slave, obeyed. The beautiful woman who was his companion, vanished; the sorcerer had removed the spell, and when Sensa looked for her he saw but a serpent which reared its head. Agmahd smiles at his fear and assures him that this favourite of the evil one will not harm the chosen servant. But Sensa cannot look on the horrible shape undisguised, and he hears its hiss of anger as he goes with averted eyes. His was the true seer's love for true beauty which is beautiful to the core. Still pleasure and rest had restored his strength, and as the "chosen servant" of the dark Queen he follows Agmahd, a deep gloom falling on him as he enters the Temple. The hour of the great ordeal is at hand, and he knows it, blinded and besotted though he is.

It will be well, before entering upon the consideration of the great ordeal, to go over the story from the commencement once more in the light of its real, vital interpretation, that of the Tragedy of the Soul. In the other two interpretations there are necessarily limitations; we are taken into the atmosphere of ancient Egypt, or into the personal life of a great adept and must remain there till the end of the mysterious narrative. How mysterious is this narrative begins to be apparent to the student only as he understands that the soul-tragedy which is so perfectly fitted into the splendid setting is literally the story of Every-Soul, of all souls that incarnate on this earth, and that it is a drama which is continually enacted from all time and to all time, in all races and countries and in all conditions. As it took place in the past, so it is taking place now, and here. To the Soul, liberation is a birthright; as it descended into matter so it must eventually emerge therefrom, freed and purified. We ourselves, and those others of the race whom we know and can observe, are at one point or at another of this universal path. In the great Sanskrit teachings the same story s told in the *Bhagavad Gītā*, where Arjuna, the Soul of man, is shown fighting upon the battlefield of his human nature. The whole of the *Gītā* bears this interpretation, while it can also be read as the story of a war. So the whole of *The Idyll* bears this interpretation, while it can also be read as the story of a seer. In both cases the story is most perfect and complete when regarded in the greater meaning, although in each case the setting in which it is so fitted as to be hidden to the ordinary reader, is true to the life of the ancient peoples from whom the Song and *The Idyll* have been drawn. The short preface, written in the same manner as the prologue, and the narrative, states clearly and concisely the real meaning of the whole.

> The ensuing pages contain a story which has been told in all ages and among every people. It is the Tragedy of the Soul. Attracted by Desire, the ruling element in the lower nature of man, it stoops to sin; brought to itself by suffering, it turns for help to the redeeming spirit within; and in the final sacrifice achieves its apotheosis and sheds a blessing on mankind.

The key to the meaning of *The Idyll* in this aspect lies in the point that Sensa, when he enters the Temple gate, enters his physical body. From that moment everything which is related takes place within himself; every person who plays a part in the drama is a personification of a quality or characteristic of his own nature. When he goes into the city for pleasure, when he appears among the people on the sacred boat, when he speaks to the people at the gate, the events are still being enacted within himself, for in each case it is a part of himself which he meets and encounters. The beautiful woman in the city is a form of his own desire; the dark goddess on the sacred boat is his own evil nature; the Lily Queen is his own divine nature. The All-mother—Isis of Egypt—who guides the souls of men to their places of birth upon earth brings him to the gate of the Temple. From the quiet fields of the unborn she leads him into the world of men, where he is at once roused and captivated by the sights and sounds of this special form of life—human life. She, the veiled and mystic Mother, comes from Eternity into Time, when she guides souls hither; and she pauses a brief moment ere her return, to gaze upon the confusion and listen to the babble, which are a part of human evolution.

She has nothing to do with physical birth, or with the raising of the Temple—when it is ready to receive the soul and come into communication with its ego, she plays her incessant and unwearying part of bringing the soul to the gate and stays until it is admitted and the gate closed upon it. We therefore see Sensa first not as a baby, but as a young boy, at the time when the awakening of human intelligence usually takes place, and that which draws him to enter the gate, that which attracts and awakens him is Ambition, personified as the high priest Agmahd.

The personification of various parts of man's nature as Agmahd and the other priests of the Temple, and as the other persons who take part in the story, is natural for an Egyptian author and characteristic of the modes of thought of his race. Professor Wiedemann of Bonn says, "the body of man throughout life was regarded [by the ancient Egyptian] as a battlefield where good and evil spirits fought for the mastery."[6]

The soul, entering into its human consciousness, is first seized upon by ambition, and under its direction surveys the possibilities of its kingdom.

It is indicated at once, by the actual movement of the story, that the mental life of man plays no important part in the evolution of the soul. Sensa, entering the "large and beautiful room" of intellectual pursuits, finds that the teacher is dim of sight, and the neophytes who study with him pay no heed to life itself and do not look upon it. He is himself the teacher and the taught; and that part of him which has worked upon the mental plane for ages has but grown blind, and the other part which studies new mental statements sees no fresh realities, but gazes only on a written page. To him, full of the craving to understand life itself, this large and beautiful room appears bare and unfurnished and he passes on through it, by command of his own wise intellect, personified in the dim-sighted old teacher, to things living and things real—the garden of life! He can only enter this part of his own nature by permission of the gardener, who has to appear before the gate can be unlocked which admits him to this "world of delicate and refreshing glory". The instinct which has led him to this gate, personified as a novice who has acted as his guide from the time of his entrance into the temple, is now strong in action, and clamours that he shall be

6   [Wiedemann 1902:14. ME]

admitted. Three times does he ring the bell before the gardener answers the summons. And when at last he slowly comes, moving among the flowers in his black robe, and agrees to receive the "new pupil" it is instinct which unlocks the gate, ushers the Soul through it and returning into the inner dimness, is seen no more.

"Come with me," says the gardener, "and fear not."

Who is this "strange man whose face would awaken interest in any human breast?"

Chapter III

The story of Sensa, is, as we are told by its author, in the preface, the tragedy of the soul of man. It takes no heed of the bodily life, or the mental life of man. Its activity and movement begin with the meeting with the gardener when the soul awakens and by its own instinct and effort reaches out beyond the walls of the temple to the mystery of that garden which belongs to it. This is not the field of open nature, but the temple garden, man's heritage, as much as the temple itself. But, though it belongs to the soul, the gardener must show the way among its beauties; Sensa would be helpless without him. Too often does the soul remain imprisoned in its temple, ignorant that there is a temple garden, for lack of demanding help from the gardener.

This is how Subba Rao speaks of the gardener:

> *Seboua*, the gardener, is *intuition*. "They cannot make a phantom of me," declares Seboua; and in saying so this unsophisticated but honest rustic truly reveals his own mystery.[7]

While Sensa is in the garden the very existence of ambition is forgotten by him. Agmahd controls him when he is within the temple walls, but not when he enters into that higher consciousness which is represented by the

7 Subba Rao 1910:240. [See p. 122 above. ME]

garden. His intuition is then his guide, and leads him to the sacred lotus tank without delay and we are at once at the heart of the mystery, in the thick of the story; the battle has begun. His own spiritual intelligence is within this garden, and by its aid he can perceive the light of the Logos—wisdom. We are shown, practically, what is waking clairvoyance, as, later on we are shown, practically, what is mediumship. By the help of intuition Sensa raises himself into consciousness in his spiritual body [the sixth principle of man according to the sevenfold constitution of the microcosm derived from Brahminical philosophy]. This spiritual being in its awakened and enlightened state is able to perceive wisdom, and therefore Sensa, the human monad, is able to hold direct communication with the Logos. Intuition has led him to the home of the Lady of the Lotus, passing by all the other flowers, drawn by the sound of the "delicate-voiced" waters. There he sees the Goddess of Truth, and endeavours to approach her; but he is not strong enough to succeed in this first attempt, and sinks down through the planes of consciousness till with the gardener's help he re-enters the walls of the temple. He does so by a different gate from that by which he had come forth—the way is now not that of instinct, but of knowledge.

And now it is necessary to consider the exquisite and wonderful mystery of the Lotus Tank.

In the astral body, or etheric double of man, there exist centres of life, or consciousness, which correspond to the nervous ganglia of the physical body. In the ethereal body, as we are taught by ancient Hindu mystical writers as well as by seers of the present day, exist centres which are known by the Sanskrit word for them *cakra* as it is difficult to convey the meaning in a single word of any modern language. A Cakra is a wheel of living fire, and as the ego develops its higher form it learns to use these psychic powers of its etheric double and then the corresponding powers of its ethereal body. As St Paul put it, having been sown a psyche it is raised a quickening spirit. The Cakra of the brain is the seventh and highest, and according to the Yogins must become living and conscious before enlightenment can be attained. Its Sanskrit name is "Sahasrāra Cakra". which means the centre of the thousand-petalled lotus—what Seboua calls "the home of our Lady of the Lotus." Subba Rao in his exposition of *The Idyll of the White Lotus* draws special attention to what he declares is the real meaning of the Lotus Tank in the garden. He says

> *Sahasrāra Cakra* in the brain is often spoken of as a Lotus Tank in the Hindu mystical books. The "sweet sounding water" of this tank is described as Amṛtam or nectar…. Padma, the White Lotus, is said to have a thousand petals, as has the mysterious Sahasrāram of the Yogis. It is an unopened bud in the ordinary mortal, and just as a lotus opens its petals, and expand in all its bloom and beauty when the sun rises above the horizon and sheds his rays on the flower, so does the Sahasrāram of the neophyte open and expand when the Logos begins to pour its light into its centre. When fully expanded it becomes the glorious seat of the Lady of the Lotus, the sixth principle of man; and sitting on this flower the great goddess pours out the waters of life and grace for the gratification and the regeneration of the human soul.[8]

---

8   Subba Rao 1910:244. [See p. 125 above. ME]

He goes on to say that the followers of Haṭha Yoga (which is the endeavour to develop the soul by psycho-physical training, such as "posture" and the regulation of the breath), believe that in the ecstatic trance known as Samādhi the soul can reach this thousand petalled flower and "obtain a glimpse of the Splendour of the Spiritual Sun". But this is a most profound and difficult effort, and is not the result of concentration, or of trance alone, but is attained through suṣumṇa (the *da'at* of the Kabbalists). This requires much physical and psychic knowledge and effort. The path of the Haṭha Yoga exits for those who are so steeped in materialism that it is necessary for them to begin by the control of the body before attempting to control the thinking principle. There are many followers of Haṭha Yoga in the present day, but unfortunately there is an indisposition to study profoundly so as to obtain the whole teaching at the fountain-head. The bits and scraps of it which are practised, such as "breathing" and "posture", partially understood and separated from the whole, are a great danger to those who attempt them. "Concentration" without due understanding and due preparation is the greatest danger of all. The follower of Haṭha Yoga who is determined to attain success by that method will give twenty years to the conquest of his body, before attempting anything further. This path is the slowest route of all to the goal. Patañjali Yoga commences with the control of the mind and thinking principle, taking for granted that the body is in subjection. But it is fully admitted by ancient writers that instantaneous illumination is possible by means of intuition. And in Sensa we have the soul which, if it has sought to reach wisdom by the weary way of Haṭha Yoga, or the lofty method of Patañjali Yoga, has left all this in the past. He is capable of absolute faith, he is a seeker after absolute truth, and therefore by the guidance of his own intuition he is able to raise himself in a flash of enlightenment, to the sacred water tank, which is the awakened organ of perception of his spiritual form; and for a moment of supreme joy, to gaze upon wisdom.

And now we come to the point where the intense and vital teaching of *Light on the Path* is needed. The uttermost tragedy of the soul, its deep degradation, may be spared the neophyte who has learned to "kill out ambition". But Sensa has not learned this lesson. Ambition is the incentive to effort for the ordinary man; it is that which brings him even upon the path. For to become an occultist is the highest ambition of man. And Sensa, who is upon the path, who is capable of instantaneous illumination, has not learned that he must dominate the qualities of human nature before he can safely enter upon the exercise of his super-nature. Therefore instead of controlling ambition he is controlled by it. Dark-visaged, unnamed instincts press upon him; they are the creatures and tools of ambition. And intuition is of no use to Sensa now. Seboua cries out, "you have seen—you are a teacher of men"—and hands him over to the instincts of the lower nature which place him immediately in the thrall of ambition.

This is a profound lesson for the neophyte, hard to learn. He does not know that until he has learned, he cannot teach. A glimpse of wisdom is enough to make him think he is a teacher of men; and his intuition leaves him helpless. From want of knowledge he fails under this first great temptation and becomes the tool of his own ambition. There are those in all ages who go thus far, and no further, who are so completely dominated by the ambition which seizes upon them that never again do they see the Lady of the Lotus. And now begins the battle—is this to be Sensa's fate? or not.

Ambition alone was not tempting enough to seize and possess the soul which had so lately looked upon the Supreme; and therefore, the high priest does not address Sensa when he comes into his presence from the garden, nor does he act alone. So soon as he has looked upon the strange face of the illumined soul he goes for his great ally, his brother, as he calls him, Kamen Baka. This high priest is clearly shown by the movement of the story to be the personification of human desire.

All the lower qualities of the man's nature now rise into activity, anxious, and determined, to obtain the mastery over the higher nature and use its supreme gift of perception for their own gratification. In some natures the cold and heartless claim of ambition for power and supremacy would have sufficed to effect this; but this soul whose history we are following is highly evolved, it is full of love of beauty and of beautiful pleasure, and therefore the priest who personifies desire is called to consult with Agmahd. Throughout the whole struggle Agmahd holds the position of ruler among the priests; and Kamen Baka, though called by him "my brother" is dominated by him. This highly evolved soul is ambitions in desire; it seeks no common or crude gratification. The lower instincts, personified as younger priests, wait upon Sensa, refresh him, and make him ready, so far as is in their power, for the supreme effort decided upon. For Kamen Baka has advised that the seer should be at once taken straight into the presence of Desire itself.[9] From her he draws his own inspiration direct, and he regards her as that which is life. Agmahd permits himself to be led by this advice, and lets the soul rest. From this rest it awakens to find itself in darkness, the awful darkness of the Temple, and

9 *Avidyā*, "the dark side of human nature" [Subba Rao 1910:244; see p. 124 above. ME]; "The first illusion and the last" [Besant 1897:407. ME].

surrounded by a dense crowd of beings animated by desire alone, and eager to use his priceless gift for their own ends. The whole of his mysterious and infinitely complex nature is demanding life and gratification, and this fierce crowd, silent in its passion takes the child in its grip, and compels him to approach the door of the innermost sanctuary of his being, the dark and awful holy of holies. The circle of priests which had surrounded his couch when he awoke, closes round him as he moves at the command of Agmahd and he passes on his way, powerless. For not only do these nearest close about him, but they are closed upon by others, and in every direction, so far as he can see, the crowd closes in. Is not this the true picture of the awakening of manhood and womanhood? The whole being arises in a storm of agitation, to demand of brief human life all that it has to give; the little spark of divinity in its midst is led hither and thither by it. And the horizon is scarcely to be seen, or the world outside remembered, for the turbulence and growing strength of all these strange qualities which go to the making of a human being. Sensa, passing to the inner sanctuary, catches a faint glimpse of the outer world he has left and it is to him like the face of an old friend. Prisoned in the microcosm he looks for a fleeting instant upon the macrocosm before he enters the deepest darkness of the tomb into which he has descended.

He is not conquered yet; he is still the unsullied soul, and the first sight of the lambent fire of Desire makes him alarmed and miserable; and when he sees its actual form he is filled with horror. Desire commands him to enter the sanctuary alone, and he neither can nor will do so. Then in anger she reveals her face to him and he shrinks with loathing and fear, falling once more into unconsciousness. Again the strain had been too great for him; the first time it was the attempt to reach the light of the Logos which was beyond his strength; now the revulsion from that which lurks in the darkness of his own lower nature utterly exhausts him. This is a crisis in life which every one experiences in himself more or less definitely, and which those who have the opportunity of watching the change from youth to maturity take place in others, are familiar with. To the one who is passing through it, nothing else in the universe is of any importance for the time being; the amazement of discovering within one's nature the great cosmic forces which form the two arms of the crucifix, at work and at war is so bewildering. That good and evil should be encountering each other on the general battlefield of human life, in the affairs of men and of nations; is comparatively easy to understand; but that this same warfare should be found within one's own small heart is at first a great surprise and a great shock. But it is so; the fact is there, the microcosm reproduces the macrocosm in every detail, and the great dark Queen of Desire who is almost visible in the midst of the carnage of a revolution is quite visible to the spiritual seer in the dark place of his own inner nature. The vision leaves him almost lifeless, helpless and amazed. When he recovers from the swoon and cries aloud in terror at the recollection of what he has seen, a priest who is in attendance upon him, a representative of his lower mentality, offers him fresh water and brings light into his room. And then he proceeds to urge upon him that he need not fear, that it is only his youth which makes him afraid, that he has received great honour, that the gaze of "our all powerful lady" is enough to make a man swoon. This priest is evidently an emissary of Agmahd's for he speaks as one who has been told what to say, and recites his lesson well. He bids the youth not to rebel against the vision, but to appreciate the honour which has fallen on him; and above all not to be afraid. The arguments brought forward by this priest are those which every soul, horror struck at the first sight of evil within itself hears from its urgent desire—nature, and the instincts attendant upon that nature. "Surely the world and all that is in it exists for the pleasure of the soul; is it not mere cowardice to shrink from that which arises naturally and which draws and leads all men?" Unable to answer such questions the weary and terrified soul looks for the help of intuition and asks for Seboua. The thought of going into the wonderful and beautiful garden of his soul rejoices Sensa, and he waits patiently for Seboua to be aroused and brought to him. Intuition does not work in the dark; it needs the light of the sun, it lives and moves in life and light and beauty. Its quickest and keenest moment is at the wonderful hour of 64 dawn; and the weary spirit must wait for the first faint ray of light before intuition is strong enough to come to his aid. Then the priest, whose words had chilled and disheartened Sensa, summons the gardener, and Seboua—"human! loving"—if uncouth and dark, comes to the sad and shadowy room where the spirit is brooding. This description of a weary and hopeless night vigil, followed by a return of courage and hope when the dawn comes, will be recognised by most people; it is a part of the common lot and general experience of man. Seboua kneels humbly beside the gifted child, who demands of him an explanation of the reason for his being horrified by the sight of the ghastly face of Desire. Seboua does not attempt to answer this question but leads him forth at once among the flowers, and when the joy of life has seized again upon the child, points out to him that in spite of the darkness and its horrors, the sun rises again and again in all his magnificence. Then he leads Sensa, unawares, to the lotus tank and asks him if he sees the goddess. Sensa is still full of fear, and dreads to see the dark and cruel face of Desire. But when he looks up the fair woman of the Lotus[10] is once again before him and he knows that intuitively he has once more reached her home. Seboua urges him to speak to her, and falls again upon his knees to watch the great event which might possibly now take place, of the opening of communication between man's higher nature and the Divine itself. Sensa attempts to approach her, again, and with Seboua's help, reaches the water tank in his higher consciousness and touches the very garment of the goddess where it falls upon the surface of the water. He tries to look into her face, but light radiates from it and he cannot see it because of its glory. He is blinded by the splendour of the Logos. The Lily Queen addresses him, and this gives him courage to ask the question which fills his soul and haunts him.

"Mother, what of the darkness?" Poor quivering human soul, asking of its own highest the question of the ages—how to deal with its own lowest. And now the Logos itself gives in plain words the grand teaching of the ages, taught always by every true philosopher and mystic.

> The darkness is not to be feared; it is to be conquered and driven back as the soul grows stronger in the light.[11]

If the darkness of man's own inner nature is not to be feared, then is there nothing in the cosmos which can strike him with dismay or fill him with alarm. For the darkness of "the innermost sanctuary of the Temple" is of the same substance as that of Hell itself. The Lily Queen

---

10 *Vidyā*, wisdom.
11 [See p. 32 above. ME]

explains to the seer, in simple language, that this innermost sanctuary of the Temple is secluded from the light of day in order that it may be illumined by the light of the spirit. It is not so illumined because the "blind priests" the qualities of man's nature which are drawn from darkness (*Tamas*) comfort themselves with its brood, and resist illumination.

These same priests, with their attendant brood of the evil thoughts of darkness, were already at work upon their task of shutting out the light of the spirit. Sensa was drawn back, in suffering, from the high place he had reached; Seboua stood rebuked and downcast. Ambition and Desire, in the persons of the two high priests, placed themselves one on each side of the soul, and made it understand that its place was between them. Thus Sensa re-entered the "gloomy gates" of the Temple, leaving the place of spiritual light and life, guarded and guided by these two ruling and dominant passions of human nature. He approaches his doom; he enters upon his term of slavery. There will be resistance—there will be veiled and fearful rebellion—there will be flashes of illumination— but from now until the final great ordeal Sensa is guarded as a prisoner by the strong qualities of his own lower nature, and bidden to serve them as a slave serves.

Chapter IV

Ambition now assumes absolute control over the developing nature, and compels intuition to remain silent, not allowing it to approach the soul. Sensa is imprisoned in the sanctuary of the Temple, guarded and watched by the crowd of lower instincts which figure as novices and priests in the drama. He is prevented from going forth into the garden, or from meeting the gardener. The composite nature, approaching maturity, demands success in its undertakings, and is coerced by its overwhelming crowd of lower instincts into measuring success by the standard of the world. Wisdom and pure spirituality are of no use to one who desires to win prizes. Intuition makes a great effort to lead the soul into the higher places which belong to it, and finding it is not able to come to the lotus tank, Seboua plucks a bloom—a flower of wisdom—and sends an emissary of his own to take it to Sensa in his imprisonment. A strange imprisonment it is, for the soul is shut in its temple by those who should be its servants, as a king might be locked in his palace by his people. Sensa receives the flower of wisdom with the utmost delight and cherishes it "as though it were the breathing form of one I loved." His great anxiety is to hide it from the alien eyes which surround him. Encouraged by the possession of this precious thing Sensa speaks boldly to Agmahd, and tells him he cannot endure the dullness and solitude of his imprisonment in the Temple. When relating this Sensa stays to tell the reader that five years later he would not have dared to address Agmahd in such a manner. Five years later he was the slave of ambition, as are so many of the great and successful of the world. They obey its dictates without hesitation. And in a little while Sensa would reach and pass through that condition. But as yet ambition does not mean all to him. He knows there are intensely desirable things in the cosmos which are outside the scope of human ambition. Therefore he speaks boldly to Agmahd, who, knowing the latent power of the human soul makes no angry reply, but places before it a great and terrible temptation, which has to be encountered by all as they pass along the path. It is early for Sensa to meet it; and fearing lest his strength should fail before so great a danger, the Lady of the Lotus herself comes to his aid. Agmahd places before him a volume bearing the title *The Arts and Powers of Magic* and tells him he need never again be lonely if he looks upon its pages. He does so, and immediately temptation, personified, appears before him and offers him freedom from his prison house. He offers to gratify any wish, and "freedom from this room" is Sensa's one desire. "Come," says the man in black, "follow me."

"No!" replies Sensa, "the high priests have imprisoned me—if I am found escaping I shall be punished."

The events now taking place must all be considered with the picture of Sensa (on this plane) as a young man entering upon life, born well in mind. Ambition directs that he shall take a high place in the world. Is he to do so, or is he to be a seer of spiritual truth disregarded and despised by men? Sensa knows well the punishment which would fall on him if he left his appointed place; the self-contempt, the regret. But the tempter does not stay to argue with him; he merely says in a tone of command, "Come! and look not back." This is the moment of greatest danger which has yet come to him. Had he obeyed the tempter implicitly soul-death must have been his lot. But his higher nature compels him to look back and see the consequences of his attempt to secure freedom, and he beholds his beloved Lady of the Lotus, and hears her voice calling upon him to return. "Lady, I obey," he murmurs, and is saved. Subba Rao, in writing of the real nature of soul-death and the ultimate fate of a black magician, says:

> [A soul may] place itself *en rapport* with a spiritual or elemental existence by evoking it, and concentrating its attention … on it for purposes of black magic and Tantric worship. In such a case it transfers its individuality to such existence and is sucked up into it, as it were. In such a case the black magician lives in such a being, and as such a being he continues till the end of Manvantara.[12]

Sensa is saved from this awful fate by his own sixth principle which comes into the very sanctuary in which the human soul is imprisoned, and calls upon it to awaken from the "accursed spell". He does so, and finds himself in his prison house, quite alone, deserted by his tempter and also by his higher self; compelled to endure his solitude and realise himself. He finds his flower of wisdom, but it is "languid". He clings to it however, and places it within his robe. By this faithful clinging to his blossom of truth he is strengthened to pass through the ordeal which follows, when Agmahd leads him blindfold into the inner holy of holies and then bids him look upon the goddess of Desire. But when he dares to gaze into the awful darkness fearing to see the face of horror, it is upon the glorious vision of

---

12 Subba Rao 1910:247. [See p. 129 above. ME]

the Lady of the Lotus that his eyes fall. She soothes and comforts him and bids him believe that he is safe, although he has been placed in "the very dungeon of vice and falsehood", because he himself has entered her atmosphere. And now she utters perhaps the most beautiful of all her speeches:

> "The royal flower of Egypt dwells upon the sacred waters, which in their purity and peace fitly form its eternal resting-place. I am the spirit of the flower; I am sustained upon the waters of truth, and my life is formed of the breath of the heavens, which is love."[13]

At her bidding the weary soul lies down to rest; and ambition's record of this great effort is contained in the one word "*Vain.*"

---

13 [See p. 49 above. ME]

Chapter V

The soul has escaped this great danger, only to be met by more subtle and deeper temptations. This is the ordained line of progress, terrible in its steady advance from one pitfall to another yet deeper.

Sensa awakes from rest, to find a white flower in his hand. Truth has remained with him; only a plucked blossom, but still a flower of wisdom. He regards it with pleasure and is happy in the contemplation of its perfect beauty. Upon this mood of content and confidence enters himself in another form, called into being by this very content and confidence.

A little girl, younger than himself and "bright as the sunshine" comes gayly into his seclusion and snatches the flower from him, shaking the water from its leaves.

Man is tempted and betrayed by his own powers, up to the very threshold of immortality.

This little girl is interpreted by Hindu students as *daiva-prakṛti*, the higher mind of man rejoicing in its perpetual youth and power, and its capacity to revel in the primordial light. The plucked bloom, separated from the root of truth, led Sensa into this greatest danger of all to the highly evolved soul and the highly sensitive mind. Subba Rao, in one of his lectures, speaking of the "little girl of the Idyll," pointed out that *daiva-prakṛti* is compared to a girl by Hindu writers and the "protean power" being superior to *daiva-prakṛti* therefore all the souls of human beings are made to be the wives of Kṛṣṇa. The little girl is the human soul upon that plane of glory and pleasure with which Sensa had established communication, and was indeed none other than Sensa himself in another state, using another form and entering another consciousness. It is well at this point in the story to recall the fact once more that it is Egyptian and emanates from an Egyptian source. Professor Wiedemann says of the Egyptian writings—"parts of the soul are treated in the texts as entirely independent beings".[14] He enumerates them as the "*Ka*"—(which is the best known, and is generally understood as the etheric double)—the "*Osiris*"[15] (the immortal double)—the "*Khou*" (the "perfect shining one")—the "*Ba*" (which was the human-headed bird, depicted by the ancient Egyptians as revisiting the mummy of the dead) and three other independent souls. These last three are often named in the tents, as the "*Sahu*" which wears the mumny wrappings, the "*Khaibit*" which is shaped like a fan, and casts a shadow,[16] and the "*Sekhem*" "the reverend form"[17] which is the transfigured and quickened spiritual being. Of these last three little is said in the tents; they belong to that higher nature of man whose functions cannot be described in words. This septenary conception of separate forms or souls, acting on different planes of consciousness and all attached to the physical form or Temple, and all engaged in working out the evolution of the ego, must be borne In mind when considering the story of Sensa. Later in the drama, when

---

14 [Wiedemann 1902:57–58. ME]

15 Professor Wiedemann says that "*Osiris*" is sometimes used for the Immortal Double, sometimes for the Ka (etheric double or astral form).

16 [The forms given in Wiedemann 1895 are as follows: ⊔ KA (p. 11); 𓅢 KHÛ (p. 43); 𓅢, 𓅢, 𓅢 BA (p. 31); 𓊃 SĀHÛ (p. 41); and 𓊃 KHAÏB (p. 42). See "A Note on the Text" below. ME]

17 [Wiedemann 1902:60. ME]

the little girl has fulfilled her task of making Sensa a man of the world, the young priest Malen appears as again Sensa himself in another form, an inner personality, a more permanent self.

The "little girl" is a favoured servant of Agmahd's; she leads Sensa into places of inexpressible pleasures and she draws him into games where as a matter of course he succeeds beyond his fellows, and *"wins all the prizes"*. Ambition stimulates the soul in this world of consciousness, and from the delightful experiences which befall the soul in that place of bliss, it returns to find itself no longer a free agent on the plane of human life. It has sold itself to ambition and desire and must obey them implicitly; the pleasures of the mind are the payment—some given already, some yet to come, for the "little girl" tells him he is to play often with the children. She tells him too that in future he is to dwell among earth-fed flowers—no longer is he to pluck blooms from the- lily of the water-tank. And his first punishment is to find himself uttering strange words which to him (the soul) have no meaning, for they appeal only to the lower nature. His inspiration, poured into him from the Queen of Desire, causes him to be worshipped, even by the most splendid of the priests. His brain is not now "frenzied with the follies of his own conceit" to use Agmahd's words, but he is obedient to the spell laid on him by Desire and his speech gladdens and satisfies the throng of priests who listen to him. All bow down before him; the novices kneel to offer him food; His room is made sweet and beautiful by bushes of earth-fed flowers set about it, and great bunches of flowers are brought to him to satisfy his love of beauty and fragrance. Agmahd stands silently within the curtains which seclude the young seer from the other priests, but Sensa is no longer afraid of him. Instead he is glad and proud, for he knows he has satisfied the demands of this cold ruler. And soon Agmahd leaves him, and the "little girl" returns. It is for her now to lead the soul in to the great ordeal. Agmahd knows that she alone can do it, and leaves her to the task, while he summons the crowd of priests to take part in the ceremonial and to prepare the couch covered with roses and hedged about with flowers. Here the "little girl" induces Sensa to play with her at ball, so that he forgets to be afraid. And when the sanctuary door opens the "little girl" leads him to it and so brings him to the dark goddess, Avidya herself. He has now been brought to her with such ga.y companionship that he is not overcome with fear, though the child leaves him. He is alone with the personification of the dark side of human nature. When the goddess draws him to her he perceives that her robe is a living thing, a drapery of coiling snakes. And then terror falls on the startled soul. The dark goddess laughs at his fear and makes her robe dim while she places her hand on his forehead. Then fear left him forever. Again he sees the living robe and beholds the serpents wreathing her body and rearing themselves about her head; but he feels no terror. Doubtless he knows now that the child who has been his merry playmate is one of those terrible serpents. She vanished as he entered the presence of the goddess, going to her own place in the queen's robe. The little girl is *daiva-prakṛti*—so is the beautiful woman of the city— they are identical, and both are himself, his own mind, and both are a part of the living robe of the dark queen. It is the souls of men who clothe and veil the presence of the queen of darkness and her living robe changes into such forms as they desire and will to have.

Sensa is worn out with this severe experience and Agmahd, in order to prevent too great a strain, allows Seboua to take him into the garden and to let him bathe in fresh water; but he is not to take him to the lotus tank. This is because he is so changed that he cannot approach the royal flower or the sacred water, but seeks his freedom from imprisonment, his rest and refreshment, in the astral fluid. Nevertheless he sees the goddess of truth, who comes to tell him that this mystic water is fed from the sacred tank; and that if instead of sinking in it he rises and kneels upon it, and by another effort rises and stands upon it, he can do so safely, it will support him. But while making these efforts he must address himself to the Logos and demand illumination. How plain a teaching this is to the many who find sufficient pleasure and satisfaction in the experiences of the astral life, and regard these as true gifts of the spirit. But to them the Lady of the Lotus will come, sooner or later, and lift them up as she lifted Sensa up. She does this though she knows that he is about to leave her; but she will not permit him to forget her utterly, and through the dark years that follow, her sweet voice sings dimly in the obscurity of his brain and her words remain with him and, as he expresses it "cast a strange light upon my wretched life." For Sensa now becomes completely a man of the world, the soul within him being entirely dominated by the two ruling passions of men, ambition and desire. In the company of his own mind, personified as the beautiful woman of the city, he drinks deep of every kind of beautiful pleasure and is utterly happy. And then when Agmahd gives the summons to the great ordeal which awaits him he sees the beautiful woman revert to the shape of a serpent of desire and is once more alone.

Everything connected with initiation is purposely veiled and obscurely stated in all esoteric writings; and so it is in this mystery-drama. But we know that the initiate must gaze into the dark face of Avidyā and upon the blinding light of the Logos. These ordeals are endured by Sensa and clearly described. He succumbs to the first ordeal and becomes the interpreter and messenger of Avidyā herself. But having been able to see the light of the Logos, he is strong enough in the course of the final great trial to make a desperate effort for true freedom and to obtain it. He is depicted as having become inhuman in his ambition and selfish in his desires; and yet the great effort is still possible. But it is only possible at the cost of life itself; Sensa dies in the struggle. The awful Ten drive him forth from his body, which dies, and the temple in which it dwelled is destroyed. It must be remembered that the ten are not homeless when the temple is destroyed. They belong to the five-fold field in which the human soul works out its evolution, and they pass into other activities in that field when the soul withdraws. Man, in his physical nature is mysteriously united with the physical universe by means of the five "*tattvas*" which enter into his com-position as well as into the composition of all that he dwells amongst.

In the light of Egyptian modes of thought it seems clear that the body of Sensa which dies is the personal individuality. This has been so degraded that it has to be sacrificed. The author of the story states explicitly that it is the story of the soul. Isis is the mother of the souls of men, not of their bodies. When therefore at the final fierce ordeal Sensa's higher nature asserts itself and he goes into the holy of holies to find the true Queen, the light of the Logos, there, he yields up the desecrated personality. "I am perception," he cries, "the imperishable soul", and at the command of the Queen-mother enters into another of his own forms. In the disintegration of his personality he watches the sparks of life disperse. Ambition flees forth with a rush to feed elsewhere; and the soul of Malen goes to soul-death. Here is a great mystery depicted but still inevitably veiled. All the names used in *The Idyll of the White Lotus* are words of Hebrew origin, belonging to Aramaic or Arabic idioms and convey ideas which help to explain the characters. Malen has in it the idea of a refuge, or retreat, or a place of recuperation. It was Malen who guided Sensa to the city in order that he should recover his strength. It appears that he was an inner-personality or soul-form which should have guided him to a place of true recuperation. Having failed in this, and led the human soul astray, Malen himself no longer lives. But Sensa can raise up his deserted form and enter into it and use it. It would seem that Malen should have been the "immortal double", for by using this form the "I", the ego who relates the story, is enabled "since then, to live, change form and live again; yet know myself through the long ages as they pass." But he does not say, or imply, that he re-enters any Temple during these long ages, or inhabits any physical body. And indeed it seems evident that he is never again a soul of man, for he clearly states that his mother[18] would not know him in his new form. He is suffering a great expiation, enduring a great loss, as the result of the terrible conflict through which he had passed and in which vital parts of his being had been destroyed. But the Queen-mother bids him arise in his new shape, and he finds he is still strong to move among men though he cannot be of them. He has survived the ordeal and is claimed by the Queen-mother as her own; and she gives him his work during the ages, of influencing the hearts of the people— and promises that he shall live to teach her truth in that "new fane that shall arise in the distance of time"—the transfigured form, the "perfect shining one" which shall be his glorified Temple when he has won full liberation.

18 *Isis.*

It must be remembered that the Egyptian held that these various entities, souls, and forms, which go to the making-up of a man, have to be reunited before the transfigured man, the "new fane" can be built. The Queen-mother explains that Malen's form is pure and unstained, although his soul is lost. He led Sensa to the city and left him there, answering for him to ambition by the sign of a jewel worn by desire. Thus he betrayed him; but he did not himself stay in the city of pleasure. The ego can use this form; but it appears as though the esoteric teaching of this mysterious part of the story is that the soul of Malen must be recovered, revived, and purified, before the "new fane" can be built.

THE SEVEN PRINCIPLES OF MAN[19]

ORTHODOX THEOSOPHICAL	EGYPTIAN	BRAHMINICAL AND TIBETAN
1 The Dense Physical Body.	1. The Ka.	1. Prakṛti.
2. The Etheric Double.	2. The Ren (name).	2. Liṅgaśarīra.
3. Prāṇa, the life.	3. The Akh.	3. Śakti.
4. The Desire Body.	4. The Ba.	4. Jīvātma.
5. Manas, the Thinker.	5. The Shut.	5. Physical Intelligence.
6. Buddhi.	6. The Sah.	6. Spiritual Intelligence.
7. Ātmā.	7. Sekhem.	7. Brahman.

NOTE: In the Egyptian Septenary Division of Man. it will be noticed that the physical body is not reckoned at all. The Ka is the astral instrument; the Ren ('name') is *the man*; the Akh the Perfect Shining One; the Ba the human-headed Bird which visits the Mummy from time to time; the Shut the Shadow cast in a life-time, represented by a

19 [Collins' original gives in the column for Egyptian Ka, Name, Khou, Ba, Khaibit, Sahu, and Sekhem. See "A Note on the Text" below. ME]

huge fan; the Sah *the man himself;* Sekhem the transfigured form.

I understand the Ka to be the astral form, the Akh to be the ethereal form; the Ba to be the spiritual form, the reincarnating ego, "The one who walks"; the Sah and Sekhem to be "I and my Father" who are one—the ego and the Logos.

—M. C.

References

Besant, Annie. 1897. *The Ancient Wisdom: An Outline of Theosphical Teachings*, London: Theosophical Publishing House.

Budge, E. A. Wallis. 1901. *Egyptian Magic.* London: Kegan Paul, Trench, Trübner & Co.

Collins, Mabel. 1890. *The Idyll of the White Lotus.* New York: John W. Lovell.

——. 1913. *The Story of Sensa: An Interpretation of The Idyll of the White Lotus.* New York: John W. Lovell.

Gardiner, Alan. 1966. *Egyptian Grammar.* London: Oxford University Press.

Subba Rao, Tallapragada (as T. Subba Row). 1910. *A Collection of Esoteric Writings of T. Subba Row*, Bombay: Bombay Theosophical Publiication Fund.

Wiedemann, Alfred. 1895. *The Ancient Egyptian Doctrine of the Immortality of the Soul.* London: H. Grevel.

——. 1902. *The Realms of the Egyptian Dead according to the belief of the Ancient Egyptians.* Translated by J. Hutchinson. London: David Nutt.

A Note on the Text

Very few alterations to the text have been made. Oxford spelling has been adhered to, which practically only involved altering the older spelling *noviciate* to *novitiate*, and correcting the errors from *would'st* and *bretheren* to *wouldst* and *brethren* respectively.

In Swami Tallapragada Subba Rao's essay I have updated the spelling of Sanskrit, Chinese, and Hebrew words to modern transliteration. I preferred *Buddhahood* to his *Buddhaship*, and corrected some OCR errors found in the Wikisource version (which I have also corrected).

In *The Story of Sensa* I have done likewise, updating some words to modern transliteration. In addition to this, I have corrected the spelling *Agmabd*, *Sebona*, and *Sancrit* (evidently persistent typesetter's errors) to the forms found in *The Idyll of the White Lotus*, namely *Agmahd*, *Seboua*, and *Sanskrit* respectively. Where Collins has "the Idyll" or "the *Idyll*" I assume she is speaking of the novel and have preferred "*The Idyll*". I revised and corrected some of the Egyptian terminology. Footnotes by me have been given in square brackets with my initials to distinguish them from Collins' own.

Since Theosophical terms may be known in their original spellings (whether or not they are accurate representations of the original terms), I have given on the following pages a list giving both forms.

Michael Everson
Dundee, April 2022

Sanskrit terms	Theosophical spelling
Amṛtam	Amritam
Arjuna	Argund (an error?)
Ātmā	Atma
Avidyā	Avidya
Bhagavad Gītā	Bhagavat Gita
Caitanyam	Chaitanyam
Guruparaṃparā	Guruparampara
Haṭha	Hatha
jāgrat	jagrat
Jīva	Jiva
Jīvātma	Javitma (error for Javitma)
Kālī	Kali
Kāraṇaśarīra	Karana Sarira
Kṛṣṇa	Krishna
Kūṭastha Caitanyam	Kutashtha Chitanyam
Kāma	Kâma
Liṅgaśarīra	Linga Sharira
Mahākāla	Mahakala
Manvantara	Manwantara
Manvantaric	Manwantaric
Māyā	Maya
Nirvāṇa	Nirvana
Patañjali	Patanjali
Prājñā	Pragna
Prakṛti	Prakriti
Prakṛtilaya	Prakritilaya
Pramathagaṇa	Pramadhagana
Prāṇa	Prana
Rajoguṇa	Rajoguna
Sahasrāra Cakra	Sahasrava Chakram
Sahasrāram	Sahasravam
Śakti	Shakti
Samādhi	Samadhi
Satva	Satwa
Satvaguṇa	Satwaguna
Sthūlaśarīra	Sthulasarira
Suṣumṇa	Sushumna
Suṣupti	Sushupti
svapna	swapna
Taijasa	Tajasa

Tamoguṇa	Tamoguna
Turīya	Tùreeya
Vidyā	Vidya
Viśva	Viswa

Hebrew term	**Theosophical spelling**
da'at (דעת)	dath

Chinese term	**Theosophical spelling**
Guānyīn (觀音, 观音)	Kwan-yin

Egyptian terms	**Theosophical spelling**
Akh (*3ḫ*)	Khou[1]
Ba (*b3*)	Ba
Ka (*k3*)	Ka
Ren (*rn*)	Name (translation of Ren)
Sah (*sˁḥ*)	Sahu
Sekhem (*sḫm*)	Sekhem
Shut (*šwt*)	Khaibit[2]

---

1   [See also footnote 18 on p. 178 above. ME]

2   [Gardiner 1966:508 (*s.v.* S35) says that the word *ḫ3ybt* was another word for 'shadow' "found in the XXth Dynasty and perhaps earlier" but its identification with or "is very doubtful". ME]